Breaking the Good Book

(a biblical novel)

also known as

The Sandwich Maker's Last Meal

© 2015 Dave Hopwood.
All rights reserved.

Other Books by Dave:

Top Stories – 31 parables retold with contemporary comments

Pulp Gospel – 31 bits of the Bible retold with comments

Film & Faith – 66 movie clips that bring the Bible to life, with questions and comments

Parables - A collection of stories to chew on. Yarns with an eye on another world

Sons of Thunder – A contemporary gospel

No More Heroes – Cain, Solomon & Jacob in a modern tale of men, women, dads and crime

Spondulix – A tale of crime, greed, guns & cash and what happens when you put them all together

The Shed – A novel. 40 days in a shed with a disgruntled guy, and the pilgrims, stragglers and wanderers he encounters

The Twelfth Seer – A novel. A big screen, action adventure; the quest for divine power

Dave is a freelance speaker and author. For more info and to receive his regular creative emails – **davehopwood.com**

Breaking Into the Good Book

(a biblical novel)

also known as

The Sandwich Maker's Last Meal

Part One
Breaking In

2

1. The Sandwich Maker

I could see he didn't believe me from the first off. The get go. Why should he? Perhaps you can only believe something like this if you're prepared to look beyond yourself, and what is 'real'. To other places. Other worlds. Other ways of doing things. Beyond your own limits. To recognise frailty, and vulnerability, and endless possibility. The realisation that we can do a lot. But not everything. To see beyond this visible world to another world, another dimension, a reality we cannot control. A reality we can only partly grasp with our flimsy earthly fingers, a world that sometimes seems as solid granite yet at other times as slippery and elusive as soap. I had been to that other place and I think that's why the tale seemed so strange when I told it in this world.

But I did my best. I sat in his old, stale armchair, the one that had no doubt housed plenty of neurotics and hopefuls before me, and I tried to tell my story. And as I talked I flicked at the moleskine notebook with my fingers, and clutched that leather pouch with those very green leaves in. He merely stood still, looking through his murky bay window.

It's hard to even begin to tell you how it came about. That's what I told him, as he continued his staring. This road trip, I said. This odyssey, if I can dare call it that. All I can say is that I'd known Aladdin Strike for the best part of three years when he took me aside in his dusty, sun-streamed apartment one day and told me about the sandwich maker. Al said that he had this friend who had been reading about these four ancient mystics who had once broken into paradise via the biblical book, *Song of Songs*, way way back. A kind of celestial breaking and entering. We're talking a long time ago. These ancient sages believed that this bit of the Good Book represented a doorway into a close encounter with the riches and mystery of God. A portico that transported any explorer across the bridge and over the cavern that stood between this world and the next. For those brave enough and crazy enough to go looking it offered the opportunity to sneak into paradise by a side door, a sort of divine fire exit. A portal for getting back into Eden in a strange mystical way. The four mystics had plotted, prayed, meditated and somehow managed the break-in. However, only one of them, a guy called Akiba Ben Azzai, actually made it in and out without going mad, dying or generally losing the plot.

And this had inspired Aladdin's friend to get all creative and start working on inventing some kind of novel chemical process, along with some kind of state-altering device, that meant he could do the same thing. This friend turned out to be an old priest of sorts. A priest, yet also a scientist, and a chemist, and a visionary. And a sandwich maker who ran his own movie-themed sandwich bar going by the name of

5

Reservoir Dog's Dinner. This extraordinary dude was now looking for a couple of young guys with enough energy and madness to want to try the trip with him.

2. Isabeth

We met late at night in the cobwebbed, dimly lit back room of the sandwich bar. It was the first time I saw the sandwich maker and he did look a little kooky. He had patches of grey and red hair sticking out of the sides of his head and clumps of auburn whiskers on his neck and chin where he had failed to shave properly. He was wearing odd shoes and only one sock, and a lab coat spattered with all kinds of potent looking stains. He could have been anywhere between 25 and 50, it depended on the light. He was kind of ageless to be honest. And weatherworn, as if he'd seen too many wars, too many hard times and too little nourishing food and friendship. He had wrinkles like scars and a frown on his forehead so deep it looked as if the information in his brain was cracking his skull to get out. Because he clearly had something else too. A kind of genius. He radiated it. It hung around him like moths on an old suit.

He also had John Lennon glasses that should have been cool but stuck out a little too far from his head like insect antennae. The lenses were so thick they might have been strong enough to channel lasers. He both terrified and inspired me. He looked exactly like the kind of scatty headed, other-worldly-minded boffin who could somehow break into an old book and enable the likes of me to walk across the vast landscapes of its wafer thin pages. So I trusted him and I didn't. He thrilled me and he horrified me. But there was little time to wrestle with that or debate with Aladdin. We were in his back room and we were handed vials of smoking green liquid, while he told us of his scheme. He had spent 18 months blending and mixing and calculating and now he figured his life's work was done. He had created the means of entering the Good Book, delving into the depths of its power and drinking deeply of its hallowed nectar. Sucking the sacred marrow from its pages. Even maybe, entering paradise itself, as the four seers had once done. That set me on the edge of my seat a little. Three of the seers had come to a sticky end. Madness, death or legend. Which closing scene awaited us the old sandwich maker couldn't say. The only thing to decide was whether we were up for the ride. Whether we were ready to find out which end was ours.

Then Isabeth Constana turned up. A young woman with sleek silver glasses and sharp red lips. Her whole being was sleek and sharp too. Cool blue eyes that could keep you so fixed, so rooted to the spot it was as if she'd grabbed you by the shoulders.

'Who's she?' I muttered to Aladdin, and obviously everyone heard me say it.

Isabeth didn't bat a cool eyelid. Aladdin shrugged, adopted a kind of attitude as if to say he'd barely noticed her enter the room. But it was clear he was smitten.

'My niece, three times removed,' the sandwich

maker mumbled.

Can you have a niece three times removed? I didn't know and couldn't ask.

'She's coming too,' was all the sandwich man added. He handed her a vial of green liquid.

'Is there alcohol in this, 'cause I don't drink,' she said, and her voice was cool like her blue eyes. I guess it could be sharp too, if she wanted.

The sandwich man shook his head. 'Alcohol should be the least of your worries with something like that,' he added. Then he grabbed a handful of spindly white cables and handed them round.

'Everyone ready,' he mumbled, more a statement than a question.

Six months ago I wouldn't have been, but now I seemed to have hit one of those troughs in life, one of those times when you feel as if you have nothing to lose. I was ready.

We drank and plugged the white wires into various bits of ourselves. Nothing too invasive, but strange enough that you wouldn't want a photo of the moment. The green smoking drink was bitter, like over-stewed tea, mixed with bad fruit and sour wine. I drank it down in two gulps, I would have finished it in one, but there was too much of it and the bite of the mixture made me splutter part way through. I just hoped that the sandwich man wasn't a madman set on poisoning us all. Aladdin turned a little green but quickly adopted his crooked grin, and that's when we plugged in, sat down and the sandwich man switched his switches. The machine he'd created was a little on the small side, certainly didn't look any kind of time and space travelling device. Not much more than an overblown toaster. It even had a couple of dials on the side, like you'd use for adjusting the length of time you wanted to cook your bread. We waited. I got bored. There was no flash, no room shuddering, no mighty wind or flash of lightning. I did feel suddenly tired, and that made me shut my eyes for a moment.

Then I felt something dust my face and I put my palm on the film of sand that had collected on my cheek. There was a breeze and I felt the gentle sting of soft, hot grit. I opened up, looked around. I was no longer crammed into the sandwich maker's back room with the others. There was no sign of Aladdin or Isabeth or the white-coated, tufty-haired madman. My head suddenly swam and I felt momentarily nauseous, some kind of travelling reaction. I sat with my head down until it abated and then I raised my eyes and looked around. Cautiously. I was sitting on the floor of a bleak barren valley, my knees pulled up to my chest. Walls of rock bordered the place and I was alone. Just me and the breeze and the sand. And a distant speck on the horizon. A moving speck. A speck that took limbs and a lilting gait as it kept walking towards me and morphed into a tiny figure. I sat and watched, my knees pulled up and my feet flat out front, the sand forming micro mountains on the top of the toes of my scuffed-leather baseball boots. The figure was a man, and as he came closer the first thing I noticed was his weird dress sense. Bright blue baggy trousers, crumpled and needing an iron, a yellow flowery shirt hanging down around his hips, not tucked in, and a tartan headband clasping his wild hair to his head. Eventually he rocked up nearby me and shielded his eyes from the sun. He looked at me then looked away. He dropped to his knees, then flopped into a twisted sitting position, looking not much more than a bundle of bright rags on the desert floor. Kind of like next week's washing.

3. Ezekiel

Aladdin and I were different. Quite different. Yet the same in enough ways to make our friendship hold together well enough to survive three years' worth of knocks and misunderstandings. I'm a shy guy, quiet, people-watching, making mental notes all the time. Instinctively. Liking one-to-ones but avoiding the crowds. Aladdin, now he was the crowds man. The entertainer, the party people person. When we'd both had enough of the crowd, me sooner than him, we'd hide away with a drink and a half hour of old jokes and laughter. And a few serious one-liners to strengthen the cement of our friendship. He's the go-to, can-do guy. I'm the yes-man, wanting to be liked, desperate to please. I guess we complemented each other. And I could have done with him right now.

I pulled out my smart phone and switched it on. Best thing to do was call him and get him over here. Doublequick. The guy in the rainbow clothes didn't look too dangerous but you could never tell these days. Nothing. The phone was a dead thing. No signal, no power, no chance of calling in the cavalry. Odd that. It had been full of juice not too long ago. I tried a few times, jabbing at the on/off button like a woodpecker on speed. No go. No good. Right now I was on my own in this world.

To break the ice with the pile of blue, yellow and

tartan washing slumped in front of me, I spoke to him. But it was as if he didn't see me. Instead he jumped up and kicked at something on the desert floor, like a sulky schoolboy scuffing at the pavement. He kicked a couple more times until something he kicked came loose and stuck up in the sand, all white and spikey. It turned out to be a bone. And not a little finger but a human rib. Rainbow-clothes-man picked it up and then crouched down and found another, and another. He mooched about and kept kicking and the more he kicked the more bones protruded from the valley floor. Eventually there was a total jigsaw of legs, arms and ribs bursting up from the ground. An army, or if not an army then a sizeable unit. The kind of crack force you could capture a building with, if they only had muscles and sinews and a few tools of the trade.

I spoke to him again. He glanced at me, then came over and stopped in front of me. He looked to the sky, and nodded. He looked my way, then back the way he'd come, then to his right and then his left. He reached out and snapped his fingers, just by my left ear. It was so close it was like a gunshot. Just as I was recovering from the resounding crack he opened his mouth and bellowed, right at me. It was loud. And I mean LOUD loud. Fortunately he twisted on the spot, spinning around and away from me as he continued spewing out his yelping. I tried to interrupt but the words just got swallowed up in the sound pouring from the other guy. The reverberations from his spinning and calling out started kicking up the sand and the ructions spread in waves away from us both, hustling the bones together in little piles. And the piles became skewed figures on the fast rippling floor, and then the skewed figures jolted as if someone had plugged power cables into them. My eyes nearly burst from their sockets as the figures sat, stood up and stared. The long dead bones found one another once again, locked into place and became their old selves. The sound dropped to silence and the skeletal unit stood stock still. All skulls and bony limbs. And as I watched the unthinkable happened. Flesh and muscle and sinew grew back onto the bones, like fast moving moss, snaking across a sea of bleached twigs. Like paint seeping through canvas to form a wholly new and original picture. The muscles and sinews and flesh weren't old, rotting and grey, as in some horror flick, but lively, pink and blood-infused.

The rainbow guy seemed anything but fazed by all this, as if he came to the valley regularly to resurrect the dead, and before long he looked to the skies and nodded again. I heard nothing but he clearly got an earful of something. His face creased into various expressions as he received instructions. That's when I noticed the wind brewing up. Rainbow guy started spinning on the spot with his arms out, as if he was stirring a maelstrom, conjuring the vortex which came thundering in from all sides. It didn't last long but the moment it died away I heard a cough. Then another. And a gasp. And the place was alive with spluttering and sneezing. And the eyes of the long-dead swivelled in their sockets as their limbs began to stretch and exercise. There was more coughing and groaning as the once-dead started kicking again. The rainbow man snapped his fingers again, another whip-crack sound, and the army immediately froze, stock still and upright. They seemed to have grown in number, the valley was full of them now. I hoped there was a mess tent nearby 'cause these guys would be ravenous after centuries without any grub.

Rainbow guy looked to the heavens again, gave another nod and turned and walked away. Just left them. No orders, no mess tent, no nothing. I ran to catch him up.

'Aren't you going to do something now?' I asked.

He looked at me as if I'd just appeared out of thin air. He scratched his head and blinked his big eyes. 'I already did something.' And he went on walking.

I gave a single glance back to the valley troops. They were still statue still and I wondered how long it might be before they faded back into the desert floor, just the same old bundle of dry bones, waiting for the next resurrection show.

'Does it mean something?' I asked.

'Of course. It always means something. But I doubt they'll notice.'

'Who?'

'This lot.' And we stopped on the brow of a small hill as he snapped his fingers and flapped a hand in the direction of a bustling city below. It was almost as if he'd conjured the place out of his imagination.

He looked at me and I noticed he had a clown kind of face, given to quick and easy expression, but with deep-set, implicitly sad eyes.

'They never listen,' he said. 'I was warned when I started the job. No one would listen he told me, and he was right. They don't. They just turn up for a bit of gleeful entertainment, something weird to watch. The local prophet putting on a show.' He shook his head. A sudden thought cross-bowed its way into my brain.

'You know you're in the Bible?' I said.

'What?'

'A book – called the Bible.'

'A book?'

'Yes…' I felt my pockets and found my old moleskine notebook. 'A book.' I waved it at him.

He took it and thumbed it with wonder in those big eyes of his. 'A book.' He said. 'A book.' The word tripped clumsily over his lips. 'A book.' He looked at me. 'This book?'

I laughed and he looked startled. 'No, that's just my notebook. The Bible's much bigger. Massive. The world's bestselling book.'

'There are other books?'

'Yes, but you're in the bestseller. You and this

valley and probably plenty of the other things you've said and done.'

'You know for a fact?'

I didn't. 'What's your name?' I said.

'Ezekiel.'

I had grown up hearing various bits of the Bible, but many of the stories had been buried under life's luggage. I was pretty sure Ezekiel was in the Good Book though. I even had recollections about that valley and the bony soldiers.

He shook his head and handed my notebook back. 'No one listens,' he said again. 'They just want a show.'

'But they will. They may not be listening now but yours is the sort of stuff that'll last forever. Maybe that's what it's about. Talking to another time.'

He went. But with every heavy-footed step he took I was sure he was in the Bible. I looked around. I didn't fancy a trip into Ezekiel's town. Not yet. I needed to find Aladdin and the sandwich maker first. I turned and picked a path across the sand.

4. Noah

There was something big in the distance, something looming out of the earth. Misshapen and monolithic. And I heard banging, growing louder with every step I took towards this strange creature. I spotted movement, a flickering at the top of the beast. Like a flame appearing then disappearing, almost extinguished by the wind then defying the inevitable and snapping back into life again. The flame grew back and more animated as I drew closer. It took a while and walking was hard with my feet disappearing beneath the hot sand with each laborious step. But eventually I got close enough to see it wasn't a flame at all, and there was no wind kicking it about. It was a man up there, appearing and disappearing, and as he did so making the banging noise I had heard along the way. I stood in the shade of this creature for a while, my hand forming a peak over my eyes as I gazed upwards towards him. Eventually I called out.

'What is this?' I yelled pointing at the monster before me.

He stopped his flickering about and looked straight at me. He shielded his eyes with a peak of his hand to get a better look.

'What's it look like?' he hollered.

'A fortress maybe?' It didn't look much like a fortress but I was being polite.

'Ha!' he laughed and snorted and disappeared again. Then he reappeared and snorted again. 'Does this look like a fortress? Why would I need a fortress out here in the desert?'

'I don't know. I was making a polite guess.'

'Well try making an impolite one,' he called back.

'A church?' I figured we were in religious territory so maybe he was making his own theatre of worship.

'What's a church?' he hollered back.

'Somewhere you go to worship God,' I told him.

'I don't go anywhere to worship God. I don't need to, I do it here.'

'So maybe it is a church then.'

Another laugh and another snort. 'It's a boat you fool.'

I leant back a little, as if somehow an extra six inches might make it all suddenly come clear. A boat? Right. 'Why would you need a boat out here in the desert?'

'I do what I'm told,' he said.

He disappeared for quite a while then I heard steps descending the huge wooden structure. For the first time, as my eyes wandered down the side of the edifice I spotted another two figures, perched in harnesses, slapping paint on the boat.

'My sons, Ham and Shem,' a voice said, 'and it's not paint, it's tar. Making the thing watertight. Not much bothered about tarting the thing up.'

It was the flickering candle. He was walking

towards me, broad shoulders, skin all tanned and tar streaks, matted long hair hanging down around the grisly frown on his face. 'We're busy as you can see, you can help or you can say goodbye.'

'This is the ark, isn't it?' I said, the penny finally dropping.

'It's the rescue boat. We call it *Salvation*.'

Even as he said this there was an almighty roar from behind me. I turned to see a torrent of vehicles washing towards us across the sand.

'Shem! Ham! Get your brother and make ready. Mister, you should pray for the ground to swallow you up right now. Falling in a hole would be good.'

I stared at him. He shook his head and snorted again. He grabbed my shoulder and hurled me towards the boat. He pointed at a gap in the structure, an aperture just big enough for the likes of me.

'What are you going to do?' I said.

'What we always do when they come, pray for deliverance.'

I ran for the boat and threw myself into the gap. I swivelled to look as the sound of creaking, rumbling and yelling rolled towards us. The sea of enemies was not far away now, and they were hurling curses and rocks in our general direction. I could just make out their faces now, warpainted with grease and mud, snarling, spitting, contorted with murderous contempt. A real rabid dog's dinner of a militia. Bits of their vomited grit snagged at my face and chest as I watched their wheels churning the sand, as bit by bit they came sailing ever closer. Carts and chariots and carriages made out of rough wood, pulled by camels and horses or pushed by huge sweating men and women. The roofs were awash with catapults and slings and these were being loaded with rocks the size of a dead man's skull. They let loose again and the ark took another pounding. Much more of this and we'd all be history. I caught sight of Noah, kneeling near the boat, his head thrown to the sky, his mouth moving rapidly. I was amazed he'd not been annihilated in the first couple of onslaughts. I threw one or two prayers up myself as I huddled in the crevice there.

Then, not long after the murderous slings had let fly a third stony tirade, there was a boom from my left and a slurry of razor sharp stones sprayed the approaching vehicles. Men and women went down, and horses reared and staggered. Animals were certainly being harmed in the making of this epic. I pushed my head out and caught sight of a second army approaching from the right. More painted men and women, faces awash with hatred, contorted mouths spewing their venomous threats. They were gathered around a colossal cannon, some of them leaning into the vast mouth and shoving in more ammunition. They loaded up, jumped clear and as the big gun boomed again a second wave of stony carnage ripped into the other army. Splinters flew and carriages and carts split apart. The catapults and slings sprang loose from their moorings and fell skewed into the sand. The opposing men and women did their best to rework their hardware and send another onslaught of rocks towards us, but their aim was off and most of the missiles plummeted into the sand or flew at odd angles past the men and their boat. The cannon boomed again and this time the attackers gathered up the detritus of their vehicles and began to withdraw. As the first army pulled back I looked to the second vicious band of rebels. They turned to Noah and gesticulated at him. For a moment they looked as if they were going to turn their firepower on us. They hissed their threats and proffered crude hand signals and began turning the gun. They eyeballed the boat and gloated with evil glee at such an easy target. But for some reason they didn't reload their cannon, instead they kept turning it and then, under instructions from a huge one-armed giant of a man, they started hauling it away. No doubt threatening to come back another day.

Game over. For now anyway. I glanced down at the rips in my clothes. A few of the rocky missiles had marked me. I heard a snort and looked up. Noah was standing near me shaking his head.

'Corrupt days,' he said, 'violence and depravity everywhere you look.'

He slapped the boat with his coarse, flat hand. 'That's why we need *Salvation*.'

He offered me the hand he'd used to slap the boat and pulled me out.

'Who are they?' I asked.

He let a jaded sigh slip from his mouth. 'Just the neighbours,' he said, 'the locals. Two tribes who've long been at war with one another. Long lost in their anger and despair, bent on destroying anything good. You want to sail with us when the time comes?'

'I get seasick,' I said.

'You'll get more than that if you hang around this place too long,' he said.

I dusted myself off and just smiled. He had no idea where I had come from, and though I didn't have the first idea what would get me back there, I knew it wasn't his monstrous boat.

'Want a tour before you go?' and he seemed suddenly cheerful for the first time. He grabbed my shoulder and let me inside his creature. It was still little more than a skeletal frame, but his imagination and fast-talking decked it out for me. The compartments and storage vaults and the gangway up the gap in the centre. 'Ideal for throwing out dung and pulling in fish,' he said, 'don't need a door on the side, it'll only be ripped off in the coming flood. Too violent. Get the animals up inside on this walkway then pull it up and hey! You're setting sail.'

I could see him now, up there with his boys, the boat heaving and rolling as the waters tore at it. I didn't envy him a single day of what was up ahead. Instead I shook his hand, thanked him for saving me from the death of a thousand rocks and carried on walking. Pretty soon I could hear him banging about again and when I turned to look back his boys were just tiny toys on the side of the monster and he was that candle again, flickering about up top. I turned again and walked away.

5. Deborah

I heard her before I saw her. The sound of her piercing laughter shook the air. Up ahead there was a clump of palm trees, a group of folks were sitting in the shade there. She was standing up, laughing and talking. Her voice had a penetrating twang to it. Her face had a fiery glow to it too, her cheeks permanently blazing red as she spoke. She narrowed her eyes at me as I approached, I decided to stay back. I dropped into the sand and let her carry on with her story.

'So she lulled him,' she was saying, half an eye still on me, 'offered him a place to rest in her tent. And all the time her mind was racing. She was no fool, no naive chattel, she was conceiving a way to nail this corrupt piece of blustering death-monger. And nail him she did.' She clapped her hands abruptly and the small crowd jumped as one. 'Never ever go camping with this woman,' she said, her eyes gleaming and her cheeks redder than ever. 'Never.' She leant forward and beckoned her audience in a little closer. 'She soothed him to sleep, lulled him into a false sense of slumbering security, then when he was dead to the world – she made sure of it. She took this.' She suddenly held up a long spike, stained a dirty red from halfway down. The crowd swooned and gaped accordingly. 'She took it and pressed it gently to his temple.' She held it against her own head. 'Then she took this,' she held up a mallet, it had red and grey spatters on the head and handle. 'She positioned the spike against the soft part of his temple then...' and she paused now, 'smack!' More crowd reaction. 'Splat! And crack! Splintering bone and brain and Sisera's very soul came spurting and spilling from his skull. End of his wicked game. No more blustering death-mongering from that worm of a man. No more evil dominance from him and his 900 chariots. Ha! What do you say to that?'

The crowd said plenty, turning to each other and spilling their horror and wonder and morbid awe. The storyteller dropped to a crouch and turned her attention back on me, her narrowed eyes weighing me up, even from that distance. She stood again.

'You!' she said, her voice coming at me like a burning arrow. 'What brings you here?'

'I... I'm not sure, ' I muttered and she laughed.

She raised a tattooed finger and beckoned me closer. I couldn't think of a decent reason to refuse. She drew me in like a magnet. Everyone turned to look, quickly forgetting the gore of the spike story and hungry for another attention grabbing subject. It was looking for all the world like I might be the one. The crowd shuffled aside as I approached, letting me through and closer to the red-faced one. I could have done without such easy access. I could have used a reason to stay back, even just a little.

'You're a stranger round here,' she said.

I nodded.

'Are you with Sisera? A lost remnant? An enemy straggler?'

I glanced at the spike in her hand. I shook my head. She held it up and laughed.

'Don't worry, we'll only spike you when you're asleep,' she said and the others laughed. 'What business do you bring then? D'you want my advice?'

'Your advice?'

'Of course. I'm holding court, what d'you think these people are here for?'

For a story about hammering a spike through the skull of a blustering death-monger, I wanted to say. I didn't.

'I'm looking for my friends,' I said, suddenly inspired. 'A happy, chatty guy in denim and a tall, cool woman in grey.'

She thought for a moment, twisted the spike in her fingers and watched it turn. Then she looked back at me.

'Ah, yes. Alad... Aladdin... Str... Strike I believe he said he was... just before he died.'

'What?'

She laughed and the crowd took their cue and laughed along with her.

'The woman was cool,' she said, 'I admired her. Strong, wise, sensible... and yes. Cool.'

'But... did you say... he's dead?' I said.

'Yes, another tent peg story.'

I tried to speak but couldn't think of a single thing.

27

She flapped a tattooed hand at me. 'I'm joking,' she said abruptly, and there was more laughter from the group.

I wasn't so sure.

'They went towards the town,' she said. 'I offered my advice but they refused it.'

'Your advice?'

'Yes my judgement. It's what I do. I don't just tell tales of death and skewering. Would you like it? My advice?'

I looked around, the crowd were staring, their eyes big saucers of light, willing me to say yes.

'Yes. Why not?' I pulled out my moleskine notebook.

'What's that?' she snapped, pointing with her tattooed finger.

'My notebook. If your... judgement is good, I guess I should write it down.'

'Write it down...' she said the words slowly, softly, as if they were extraordinary to her. Then she went on, 'You're a scribe? A scholar?'

At last it was my turn to laugh. 'Of sorts,' I said. 'Though I doubt my words will last as long as yours.'

'How d'you know about that? How d'you know about anything lasting?'

'Believe me, I know.' The truth was too complicated. 'You'll be around a long time.'

She dropped to a crouch again and considered this.

'You're a strange one,' she said and she closed her

eyes. I waited. We all waited.

She smiled to herself and began humming. She laughed and began humming a little louder. The people seemed to know it and started joining in. I thought it might all be over, my audience with her. I began to back away. She was singing now, about Sisera and spikes, freedom and victories won. Then, just as I was turning to head off she stopped, stood up and spoke.

'May those who love God rise like the sun at full strength,' she said, her voice more penetrating than ever. I looked back at her. 'Guard your heart, sir,' she said, 'this journey you're on is more than experimentation. More than pages in your notebook.'

I frowned at her, then scribbled in the notebook. She, meanwhile, sat down and started drawing in the sand. I heard mutterings from the group as they deciphered her picture. I twisted my head so I could make out the image. It was a sketch of a bridge with a stickman standing on it.

6. Joshua

I left the ruddy-faced woman and her court under the palm trees. One of her crowd handed me a leather flask of water as I went, along with a ragged bundle of cheese, dates and bread. I ate and drank as I walked. The landscape was barren and I had plenty of time to mull on her message. You know how figures approach out of the heat in movies? Shimmering images all blurred and shuddering as they grow bigger on the screen. Well that was how he approached me. Totally out of focus at first but growing in size with every step. I couldn't see him clearly but something about him told me he was military. Armed most likely.

I stopped eating and stuffed what was left of my food in my back pocket. It was a struggle, the bundle was still chunky and my pocket was slight. I held the canister of water like it was a weapon, an extension of my clenched fist. We both walked on. I don't know why I didn't try and duck the meeting, take a sideways turn and run another way. But I didn't. I saw the apparition and I just kept going. I say apparition, but the closer he came the taller he and his shadow grew. And I figure that apparitions don't have shadows so he couldn't have been a figment. We stopped about ten steps apart. He was wearing the shiniest armour I had ever seen, and a huge sword hung from his side. There wasn't a speck of dirt or sweat on him. Unlike me. We stared at one another. He said nothing. I took a swig from my flask, I couldn't think of anything else to do. It was getting empty now. A few drops of water cascaded down my chin as I snatched it away from my lips. I thought for a moment then offered it to him. By the size of him I figured he'd easily drain it. He didn't move. He seemed to be waiting for something. Then the steps came. He didn't look but I did. I turned sideways and saw another soldier approaching. Shorter but still tall and broad shouldered. He stopped at an angle another ten paces away. We made a triangle, standing there in the sun and I couldn't help but think of Spaghetti Westerns.

The newcomer sighed and sniffed. He wiped his forehead with the back of his hand. He looked tired. And thirsty. I offered the flask. He took it and drank the contents down.

'Are you in this too?' he asked, handing the flask back to me. He sniffed as he said this.

'In what?'

He sniffed again. 'This. This stand-off?'

I looked at the towering warrior, his armour gleaming and shedding light all over me. And I looked at the other guy, his face grey, his eyes dark and baggy, his uniform covered in a film of dust.

'I'm just looking for someone,' I said.

'So am I.'

It was the first time the warrior had spoken and his

voice was extraordinary. Like a bunch of voices speaking in harmony. The soldier and I flinched at the sound. The warrior turned and gave his full attention to the bedraggled soldier. The soldier licked his lips, swallowed and squared up to the gleaming warrior. The warrior didn't respond. The soldier had a short sword jammed into his belt, I noticed his right hand starting to twitch, moving a little towards it, the fingers flexing and stretching. Still the warrior didn't move. Nothing was moving and there wasn't a single sound now. Just that of my shallow breathing. The warrior stared at the soldier. The soldier held his gaze. My eyes flicked from one to the other.

'Whose side are you on?' the soldier asked suddenly, and I opened my mouth to tell him, then realised he wasn't talking to me.

'Neither,' said the warrior, the sound of his voice bigger and broader than ever, 'I am commander of the heavenly forces. The question is – whose side are you on?'

I've never seen anyone move so fast. The soldier hit the ground like a rock. His body splayed and flattened. His sword skewed out from his body at an odd angle, the point embedded in the sand. I wondered if I was supposed to join him on the ground. I started to lower myself down.

'What do you want me to do?' the soldier's voice was muffled now, his lips pressing into the dirt.

I froze, halfway between standing and crouching. It

wasn't easy, I hoped the answer would be quickly forthcoming.

'Take off your shoes, you're on holy ground.'

That I could do. I didn't bother checking with the soldier, I just steadied myself and tore off my leather baseball boots. My right sock had a hole in the toe. I wondered if that would be okay. The soldier had removed his footwear too. Sandals. There was no burning bush but we both crouched there shoeless, like Moses before God.

'Who are you looking for?' the warrior asked, his voice a little softer now.

I looked up. Was he talking to me? He was looking at me. I chanced it.

'My friend. Aladdin Strike.'

He weighed this up, it seemed somehow ludicrous to be asking a giant in gleaming armour if he'd come across my reckless friend. He thought, nodded and raised a long arm. There was a string of faces tattooed on it. A lion, an ox, an eagle and a man.

'Keep going, you'll find him.'

I nodded and thanked him. Should I go now? This moment?

'Joshua and I have business to discuss,' he said, indicating the soldier. 'There are battles to be fought. Decisive battles. Invisible battles.' He nodded at the soldier.

The soldier sniffed, wiped his mouth with the back of his hand and gave me a restrained smile.

33

I scooped up my boots. Should I put them back on here or wait till I'd left? I figured I'd do that. I went and as I walked my flask felt suddenly heavy again. I opened it. The thing was full of fresh water.

7. Abram

I walked and drank and walked some more. I tried to follow the line the warrior had pointed out but I wasn't really sure. Navigation has never been my strong point. When my legs were done I sat down and decided to wait for the sun to set. That would bring shade and the cool night, and that might bring some sleep. I was fed up of walking and getting nowhere. This was like the hunt for the lost cause. No sign of Aladdin or Isabeth or the old magic man. I'd had it. My stomach growled at me and I growled back. The sun was taking forever to set. I waited, and I shaded my eyes with my hand as I studied the skyline. I guess a watched sun never sets. It was like it had moved so far and given up. Like me.

Then I began to pick up the sounds of battle. Something was going on over the far ridge. I should have noticed it before but my hearing is not great and these things take me a while. I got up and walked again. As I crested the ridge I saw them. A force of about 300 battling a disparate bunch of raiders. The raiders were losing and the 300 were beating them back. Swords and spears cut the air and sliced through bodies. Riders and footsoldiers grappled and fell, then got up and grappled some more. There was the clank of metal colliding with more metal and the sickening crunch of blade on bone. Men fell and the raiders withdrew. As the valley fell silent I noticed the general, a guy maybe in his 80s, mopping his brow and patting his men on the shoulders. They gathered up their wounded and then made for a nearby cave. There were bodies in there, cringing and buckled together. The soldiers piled in and I feared the worst. But there was no need, they tore at the bonds and set the prisoners free. The old man with the sweating brow grabbed at a younger guy and hugged him. They talked and laughed and the young guy looked mightily relieved. The general stepped away, issued a few commands and started walking towards me. I hoped he was feeling friendly. He stopped when I stood up. My stomach growled again, he was close enough to hear and laughed.

'You looking for a feast?' he said.

I shrugged. 'I'm not after a fight,' I quickly told him.

He was tall, with a stoop, and thin silver hair down to his shoulders. His eyes were grey and a little bloodshot. He laughed at my comment.

'Neither am I,' he said, 'I've had one battle today. That was enough.'

'Who were the prisoners?' I said. 'In the cave there.' I waved towards the valley where the soldiers were busy helping the men and women to freedom.

'My nephew's people,' he said. 'Invaders won a battle and came looking for their spoils. I couldn't let them ride off with my family. Not flesh and blood.'

'Abram!' A big voice called out behind me.

I swivelled to see a broad, barrel-chested king riding towards us. He was in a sedan chair, carried by four well-muscled slaves. A fifth waved a gold leaf palm branch by the king's face to fend off the heat.

The general bowed his head a little, just a subtle movement. I figured I'd better too.

'Melchizedek,' he said. 'King of peace.'

'And peace be with you also. I heard of your victory.'

'News travels fast.'

'It does when you have men watching the progress.' The king laughed and indicated to his slaves to put him down. He eased himself out and came towards us.

'Who's your friend?' he asked. Then he looked alarmed for a moment. '*Is* he a friend?'

Abram shrugged. 'He's not an enemy.'

My stomach growled again.

'And he's hungry.'

The barrel-chested king clapped his hands. 'Good – I came prepared. I have this for you.'

One of the slaves, a short, frowning man with a scar on his cheek, reached inside the sedan chair and withdrew a gold casket. He brought it over and opened it for the king to see. Melchizedek looked inside, sniffed, nodded and gestured towards us. We came closer.

Abram whistled softly. 'I'm honoured.' he said.

'Only the best from one man of God to another.

Your victory came from on high today. You know that? I'm a priest as well as a king you know? It gives me insight.'

'I know. A rare thing. A very rare thing. A king and a priest. I bow again.'

He bobbed his head and put his hand on my shoulder so that I bobbed my head too.

Then the king went into a moment of reverie, delivering something between an accolade and a blessing. 'Blessed be Abram by God Most High, Creator of heaven and earth. And blessed be God Most High, who has helped you conquer your enemies.' He paused, his expression sombre, before allowing his face to crack into a grin. 'Now, let's eat.'

He clapped his hands again and the frowning slave cast a gilt-edged rug. Somehow he managed to lay it perfectly in one swooping movement. Melchizedek sat cross-legged and we joined him. He took fine wine and fresh bread from the casket. It didn't look much yet it fed us all and we had food to spare.

'Bread and wine – life and freedom!' Melchizedek said, raising his cup and toasting us with a kind of Brian Blessed swagger.

Abram struck the king's cup with his and waved for me to do the same.

'To the king and priest,' Abram said and I repeated it.

Melchizedek nodded in appreciation. Then he laughed and slapped me on the back. I spilled my wine. Just a little.

'Don't look so serious my friend! And where d'you get those outrageous clothes?'

I looked down at my jeans and shirt. They seemed nothing much to me. The shirt had a pattern made of tiny Tintin and Snowy faces.

'It's Tintin,' I said.

They both narrowed their eyes and grimaced.

'Tintin,' Abram said.

'You know, the Belgian detective. *Herge's adventures of Tintin.*'

They shook their heads. 'Are these people in Salem? Hershay and Tintin?' Abram asked Melchizedek, but the king shook his head.

'Must be from Egypt,' he said. 'Are you Egyptian?'

I must have looked startled for they both laughed.

'Never mind,' said Melchizedek, 'if they're friends of yours then they're friends of ours.'

After that the two men got sucked into their own conversation about Abram's nephew and local politics. I sat it out for a while then excused myself, bowed one last time to the king of peace and went.

8. Rizpah

I decided to get out of the desert and a mountain obligingly appeared before me. I took the winding path and started up it. Vultures screamed and circled in the sky overhead. A picture flashed into my head of my lifeless corpse draped across the path, the birds tucking into an early lunch, arguing perhaps over the few choice bits they could find about my person. It put me in mind of that dark, recurring dream I kept having and I shuddered and shook it off. I climbed on. Tiny hills of goat droppings littered the path, and I wondered whether anyone provided *poo bags* for the farmers to use, so they could follow behind and scoop up handfuls of the stuff. I think I was getting delirious. I took another swig of my drink. It was getting low again.

Seven bodies, upright and dotted on the plateau in front of me. Not a single one moving. Then I noticed the stakes, and the dried blood, and the empty sockets. A vulture crowed above me and swooped down, landing on the head of one. And that's when I saw her. The woman with the stick and the heart of gold. She leapt at the scavenger and beat it away. As it flew up she grabbed a handful of dried goat's droppings and hurled it after the creature.

'Hello!' I called and she turned, looking both hurt and embarrassed.

She leapt in front of the impaled body and held her

arms wide. A smoking cheroot hung from the side of her mouth.

'You can't have him,' she said. 'Or him.'

She nodded towards another of the bodies. These were the only two with eyes still in their head. Now that I looked closer I could see these two corpses were cleaner, less damaged than the other five.

Another bird of prey swooped low but never made it, she caught its wing with her stick and it screeched and fled skyward. She cursed at it. Then looked back at me. She looked tired and drawn, as if it had been weeks since she had been anywhere near a bed. She was burnt too, the sun had done its work on her skin, up there in the summer.

'Why?' I said, looking around at the bodies.

'You don't know?' she said. She sucked on her cheroot and closed one eye as the smoke trailed up past her face.

I was genuinely surprised. Why would I know?

'Saul,' she said, 'that two-faced mongrel monarch. Promised the Gibeonites peace then slipped in the back way with war. Stirred up no end of trouble. And my boys paid the price. Political victims.'

I shook my head. I had no idea what she was on about.

I offered her my flask. She hesitated, licked her lips, then took it and drank. She drained it.

'Are you looking after yourself?' I asked.

'I'm looking after my boys,' she snarled, 'till the

king decides they deserve a decent burial.'

'You mean King Saul?'

She laughed, a dry-throated bitter laugh. 'Saul's long out of breath,' she said. 'My *devoted* husband took his last look at the land of the living a while back.'

'You were married to him?'

'Of course. These are his boys. That's why the Gibeonites wanted them dead. Have I got to explain everything? Gibeon made peace with Israel way back. Joshua honoured it and protected them. But when Saul came along he didn't like the idea of having foreigners on his patch, so he upended the agreement and tried to slaughter them all. He failed but they never forgot it. So when the shepherd got the throne the Gibeonites asked him for seven of Saul's boys as compensation. Here they are. Sacrificed and exposed. King David's peace offering. But I'm hanged if I'll let my sons be savaged by birds and wolves. I'm staying here to guard them till the king does right.'

She sucked on her cheroot again and threw it away. 'I lost them,' she muttered, turning and wiping her hand gently down the shoulder of her nearest boy. 'My gorgeous boys. Stolen. Because of blame and retribution. What does it solve? There has to be another way. Kings always do this. I've seen it time and again. They settle old scores and wipe the kingdom clean of any previous enemies who might threaten them. Blood, blood, blood. I pray for a king who'll be different. A king without condemnation in his veins.'

She dropped to the floor and searched inside her pocket. She pulled out another cheroot and lit it.

'I'd offer you one but it's my last,' she said, the smoke snaking upwards like a burnt offering. 'And I think I need it more than you.'

I looked across at the other five corpses. Dead men without a chaperone. They were a mess. A serious sign of humanity cut adrift.

And it made me think of that bridge. The one I'd visited on a desperate night in my real life, away from this odyssey. For a moment I was back there, peering into the abyss.

'It might kill you,' I said, dragging myself back into her world.

'What, these?' she pulled out the cheroot and looked at it.

'No. Being up here. In the sun, with no water or food. What are you doing to survive? Where's your shelter?'

'I have a blanket for the nights,' she said. 'And sometimes passing birds drop bits of food too heavy for them to take to their nests.'

'You're kidding.'

'What?'

'You're joking?'

She shrugged. 'The ravens fed Elijah at Kerith,' she said. 'God sees it all. He honours those who honour him, you know.'

I pulled out the last fragments of food, still wrapped in the rag. I gave the bundle to her.

'Where's the nearest well?' I asked.

She pointed past her down the other side of the mountain.

'I'll get you water,' I said.

'You're kind.'

I shrugged and went past her. The well was down the mountain a good way. As I stumbled down I wondered what it was like to spend a night with seven dead bodies. Seven impaled bodies. My imagination was too great, I'd not stand it. Those eyeless sockets and rotting limbs. I'd be out of there, fast fast fast. I found the well and then realised my stupidity. There was no bucket. I had only the empty canteen. No rope, no means of reaching down inside. I stood staring into the abyss of the watering hole. I was thirsty myself now, the inside of my mouth turning to sandpaper. My tongue felt immediately thick and heavy. My saliva was like glue in my mouth. I had sweated too much coming down the mountain, lost vital fluid. So much for my attempt at being the Good Samaritan. My head swam a little and I felt nauseous, then the hand clamped my shoulder. A woman with a bucket in her hand smiled at me.

'You might need this,' she said.

She had short black hair, a round face and was easily taller than me. She offered me the bucket and a length of rope. I took them. She winked.

'God sees,' she said, and she turned and walked away.

After she'd gone I thought of a fistful of questions I could have asked, *should* have asked. But it was too late. Head got in gear too long after the event. I tied the rope to the handle of the bucket, lowered it down and scooped up more water than my flask could hold. I drank some of the excess then tipped it back. I was walking away with the bucket in my hand when it felt as if the tall woman had grabbed my shoulder again. I stopped, looked at the bucket. I guessed it might be better to leave it for the next dry-throated traveller. I put it by the well and went back up the mountain.

I handed the flask to the woman with the big stick and the heart of gold. She was finishing up her last cheroot, and coughed at me.

'Don't suppose you have any more of these firesticks?' she asked.

I shook my head.

'Thanks for the water,' she said and she held out her hand. 'Rizpah. I'm Rizpah. Wife of King Saul, which should make me a queen, but I never felt like one.'

I looked at her hand, it was greasy and stained. I reached out to take it, but then she looked up at the blazing sun and pulled it away to shield her eyes from the glare.

'They say it stood still for a day you know,' she said, pointing up, 'that sun.'

'What d'you mean? When?'

'When Joshua needed more time to defend the Gibeonites. The battle raged on and he prayed that the day wouldn't end. So the sun stayed high, gave him more hours of daylight to win the battle.'

'You're kidding me.'

'Kidding?'

'Joking.'

She shook her head. 'God must have been in it eh? Protecting the Gibeonites with a miracle like that.' She turned and gazed at her sons again. 'Wish he'd have looked after my boys. They hadn't waged war on Gibeon.' Silence fell around us for a moment like a cold embrace. Then she spoke again. 'But it's not always the way, is it? Often evil prospers.'

She stroked the dead hand of her son. A vulture came low then thought better of it.

'Thanks,' she said, looking at me, 'thanks for stopping.'

I shook her hand, wished her the best and went. She took up with her stick again and beat off two more predators. Halfway down the mountain I realised I was in fact the next dry-throated traveller at that well and I scooped another load of water with the borrowed bucket. I drank plenty, and threw some over my head and face. I had nothing to carry it in so I wanted to be well lubricated. When I went I still left the bucket behind.

9. Ruth

They were sitting by the side of the road. One old enough to be the other's mother. And beautiful with it. Scowling but beautiful. The younger woman was smiling. Not a beauty but smiling. And her eyes showed she had spirit and strength. She held my gaze as I approached. I stood in front of them. They were both dirty, and they didn't smell great. Beauty and dirt, spirit and strength. It was a strange mixture.

'D'you have some money, sir?' the younger woman asked, but the older one slapped her outstretched hand down.

'Not that,' she hissed, 'we haven't come to that.'

'Come to what? We're helping him.'

'Helping me?' I said.

'You need to worship, don't you sir? We need money. We're giving you the chance. Giving to the poor is an act of worship, isn't it, sir?'

I dug into my pockets and found coins, I didn't figure they'd be any use in this strange world but I handed them over anyway.

The younger woman smiled again and stood up. She held up the fistful of coins and waved them about. 'A godly man, giving to the poor, praise God for a godly man like this. Bless you, sir. God honours you.'

I looked around. There wasn't a soul in sight.

'No matter,' she said, 'God hears us. And he sees

you with your kindness.'

I wished I'd given her more. But the old woman just went on scowling.

'Where are you going?' I asked.

'Back,' the older woman mumbled out of the side of her mouth, and the word came out as if she was spitting an olive stone. 'I told her to go home but she's a fool, she won't listen. And if she thinks I can give her another husband she's mad. Look at me. As dry as an old twig.'

She coughed and spat in the dirt. It was not a good colour.

'I'm Ruth,' said the other woman. 'This is my mother-in-law, Naomi.'

'Mara!' the woman snapped, 'I told you, it's Mara now. Forget Naomi. It's Mara.'

Ruth leant into me and whispered, 'It's Naomi, sir.'

I liked her. She didn't smell great, but then neither did I. She had a warm smile and I quickly decided I liked her.

'She's a foolish girl, don't listen to her. She's made a rash promise and is no doubt regretting it already.'

'What promise?'

Ruth's cheeks coloured. 'It wasn't rash... it isn't rash. It's what I choose.'

'She swears she'll stick with this bitter, old woman,' Naomi said, 'whatever happens. And look at us, we have nothing.'

'You have your farm back home,' said Ruth, 'that's

where we're going.'

'Probably overrun by squatters since we left,' she said, her voice sour with cynicism, 'and no doubt anything good from it has been pilfered. Plus there'll be gossip to high heaven when they see us coming. And none of them will lend us a hand. You could die girl, and I don't want your young blood on my hands. And I've already told you, it's no use waiting for me to produce another man for you to marry. My name's not Sarah and there's no Abraham in my life. No man at all.' She shook her head and spat into the dirt again.

'I'm not leaving you,' Ruth mumbled, 'so it's no good shouting at me. Where you go I go, wherever you live, die and worship, that's where I'll be. For better or worse. And I'm tired of this conversation now. Look, there's some water over there, I'll fetch some for that 'bitter' mouth of yours.'

I followed her.

'Wow, that's quite a promise you made,' I said.

'No it's not, it's just life. We've had good days and now we're facing difficult ones. But I believe in her God, even if she's angry with him. There'll be a way.' She knelt and scooped up water.

'What happened to you?' I asked.

'My husband died, and so did his brother. Naomi was already a widow for ten years by then. So we lost all the men and found ourselves with nothing. We're broke. Completely. But she still has the farm she left back in Bethlehem. She and her husband left it when a famine hit and times got hard and that's why she thinks they'll all laugh at her when she goes back. Returning with her tail between her legs.'

'I wish I had more money to give you,' I dug into my pockets again but they were empty now.

'You've been kind enough. The famine in Bethlehem has gone now. I'll find work and food. We'll be all right. And Naomi will smile again.' She smiled at me herself then. 'One day.'

'You're obviously an optimist,' I said.

She shrugged. 'Things have been all right so far.'

'Things have been all right? But you lost your husband!'

She nodded. 'I miss him, he was a good man. And he loved me, I mean really loved me. Respected me and treated me with dignity.' She filled a small pouch with water and stood up. 'Perhaps I'll find another good man, with God's help,' she said.

'I'm sure you will. I'm sure things will turn around for you.'

She nodded and took the water back to Naomi. I watched her walk away from me. Why had I been so sure? Something inside had urged me to encourage her, but it was easy to talk. They could have been nothing more than empty words. What did I know? I racked my brain for memories of Ruth's story but the connections were not working. I knew she was vital in some way, but more than that? I envied her can-do attitude. Aladdin was like that. Seeing life as a bunch of good opportunities, whatever the weather. I watched her hand the water to her mother-in-law. She turned back and gave me another smile, then they started on their way.

10. The Animal

I was nearing a town, or maybe even a city, the desert road was broadening out, turning into a well-trodden highway. Just as well, the night was starting to make its presence felt. I picked up speed and started jogging. If I hurried I'd find a bed before the dark found me. That's when I ran straight into the donkey. The creature just careered into the road, straight in my path. I found myself chesting its backside. Bouncing off its rump and sent sprawling back into the dirt. The donkey stopped, raised an eyebrow and snorted at me. I looked around, expecting to see a couple of locals come chasing after the beast. Nothing. Silence. Apart from another snort from the animal. I climbed to my feet, beat at my backside to get the dust off. The donkey snorted again and it almost sounded like a laugh. I went closer and studied him. He looked back at me.

'Get out of here,' I said, 'go on.'

The donkey looked beyond me, back up the road into the desert. He shook his head.

'Well... get back into town,' I said. I was running out of options here.

He stared back at me. Blinked. He twisted his head sideways, like a dog summing me up.

I gave up and walked past him. Or tried to. He sidestepped and blocked the path. It was a deft manoeuvre, one I didn't expect from a creature like this. I stepped the other way. So did he. We tried this a few times and the thing was turning into a choreographed dance.

'All right, enough of this,' I said. 'I'm in a hurry.'

Astonishingly he sidestepped and left the path open for me. It was almost as if he understood me.

'Thanks,' I said, uncertainly.

I stepped past him and headed for the city.

'That's okay,' said a voice.

Finally, someone came to claim the beast. I swung round and looked back, expecting to see his owner standing there apologetically. The donkey was alone. I spun around in a circle looking for the owner of the voice, so did the donkey. I looked at him, shrugged. The creature snorted. I shook my head as I turned and walked on.

'Where you going?'

I stopped. That same voice. My heart sank as I looked back. The animal was still alone. It cocked its head to the left again. Someone was messing with my head.

'Where are you?' I called into the semi-darkness. Nothing. The donkey looked to left and right as if waiting for a response.

'Come on!' I yelled. 'Enough of this now.'

Nothing.

I sighed and turned away again.

'You're not expecting to get in that city are you?'

This time I spun round as the voice was talking,

and what I saw made me stumble backwards and trip over my feet. Again I was sprawling on the floor. The second time in a few short minutes.

It was the donkey. I swear, the donkey was talking to me.

'It's under siege,' he said.

'How on earth are you doing that?' I asked.

'Doing what?' The donkey looked to his left and right around again as if I'd asked him how he was hang gliding or something.

'Talking! How are you talking? Donkeys don't talk.'

Even as I said this I knew it wasn't strictly true. I mean – I'd seen Shrek and the many sequels. But that was a movie. The donkey sighed and his lips flapped at me as he let the air out noisily.

'It's unexpected I know, but I come from an unusual family. Never heard of Balaam?'

I shook my head.

'Nobody ever has, and I guess his donkey's out of the question too?'

'Look,' I said, scrambling back up, 'this conversation is not happening. This ain't Narnia or Harry Potter.'

'Harry who? Is he a prophet?'

'No. Look I'm heading for a warm comfy bed, if anyone asks if you've seen me, make like a dumb animal okay?'

I began walking again.

'You'll regret it.'

I turned back. Again. 'What?'

'That city is under siege, I kid you not. Look, see those tiny creatures buzzing around the walls? They're not tiny creatures. They're Babylonians. A right blood-thirsty lot.' He flapped his lips at me, making a noise more like a camel than I might have expected. 'Go up to them and wish them a good evening if you like, but it'll be the last good evening you ever have.'

'You can't talk like this,' I said again.

'Would you like me to do it in Morse code?' he flapped his lips again making a series of short and long snorts, a few traces of donkey spit landed on my face.

I looked back at the city and backhanded the spit off as I twisted.

'Setting aside for a moment the fact that as a donkey you cannot talk…'

'I can.'

'You cannot.'

'I can.'

'NO!'

I held up my hand as he was about to argue again. 'Setting aside that small fact,' I said, 'how do you know that the city is under siege?'

'I come from good stock. I told you – an ancestor of mine saved the life of a prophet called Balaam. We not only can talk, we see angels too.'

'Angels?'

'Yup. In the case of Balaam there was a huge great guy with a killer sword just waiting to decapitate him for rebelling against God.'

I looked around. 'No one like that around here now, is there?' I hadn't exactly had a life of kind words and good behaviour.

He snorted and shook his head.

'You know something?' I muttered to myself, walking a few steps away and slamming my palm against my forehead. 'I cannot believe I'm asking a talking donkey whether there are any invisible angels hanging around waiting to cut my head off. I cannot believe it. This is madness. What's happening to me?'

'My ancestor took a beating before Balaam realised he was telling the truth, we're a patient family,' he said. 'It goes with the territory.'

'The territory?' I said looking back at him. 'What sort of territory throws up this sort of thing? *Alice in Wonderland* country?'

'Well… you are making your way across the pages of an ancient book,' he said.

'You know that?'

'Yea, but you should know it's the Bible, not Lewis Carroll. Written by at least 40 authors, none of them Lewis.'

'You know Lewis Carroll wrote *Alice in Wonderland*? How? How? How do you know that?'

'Oh we're brighter than you think. I'm halfway through *Anna Karenina* at the moment, though I have to say, it's no *Chitty Chitty Bang Bang* is it?'

'I don't know, I haven't read either of them.' A crazy thought bounced off the walls of my mind. 'How d'you turn the pages?'

'What?'

'You've got hooves. How d'you turn the pages?'

'Don't need to, I have a Kindle.'

'A Kindle? A Kindle? I don't believe this. I'm inside a paperback talking to a donkey about e-readers.'

'It's not a paperback. I think you'll find it's leatherbound.'

'Shut up! Stop it! Stop being... more informed than me!' It was all I could think of to say right then. He was clearly my intellectual superior. Even if he did smell like a dumb animal.

'That's harsh,' he commented, 'I'm hardly dumb. But that, by the way, is not the reason a donkey can save your life. Anything can honour God you know.'

I looked back at the city. Smoke was rising from small clumps of the tiny distant figures. It did look like an army biding their time, squaring up for an attack.

I swallowed my pride. 'Okay, okay,' I said, pacing short lengths as I spoke. 'Tell me this then. Should I go round the city?'

The donkey waved me aside with a wag of his head. I stepped out of his line of vision. He thought for a moment, at least he looked as if he was thinking for a moment. There appeared to be a subtle narrowing of the eyes.

'I think we should find a little side door,' he said. 'Come on.'

He led the way off the main path and cut a way through the undergrowth. I made sure no one was following, as much for my dignity as my safety, and then I followed.

He ducked and dived, this way and that, dodging bushes and trees and doing his best, it seemed to me, to lose me. Somehow I kept up and when he came to a stop, snorting and puffing, we were on the far side of the city, much closer now. There were less soldiers round this side and I spied a shadowy gap in the wall.

'See that opening, follow that for a while and you'll end up in a courtyard.'

'How d'you know that?'

'I told you, we see things, not just angels. Another dimension altogether. It's what talking donkeys in my family do.'

When they're not reading classic novels on e-readers.

'Will I get out again if I go in?'

He thought for a moment.

'I guess so. Look for a broken door and a water trough. That's after you've visited the well.'

'What well?'

'You'll see.'

He turned and disappeared into the bushes.

'Thanks,' I called after him, then I felt foolish as it looked for all the world as if I was speaking to nothing but the night. Mind you, no more foolish perhaps than speaking to a talking donkey.

11. Jeremiah

The darkness was falling fast now as I slipped inside the gap in the wall. I stopped and listened in the narrow gloom, making sure no one had spotted me cross the open ground outside the city. There had been groups of soldiers out there talking and drinking and playing dice round the fires. I had kept low and maintained as much distance as possible. In the narrow passage through the wall I waited and heard no one. It appeared I was safe. I moved on and followed the winding passage. It was longer than it should have been considering the thickness of the wall, and it reminded me of a tunnel I'd once scrambled through at a fairground. Eventually I came to the far end and a pile of rocks. Looking over them I could make out some kind of torchlit yard. The rocks partly blocked the exit, but I clambered over with some embarrassment and difficulty, and scrambled down the other side into the courtyard. A few lamps flickered and lit up random parts of it. I decided to head straight across and out through a far gate. I steeled myself and ran for it.

I was in the dark. I had admittedly been in the dark ever since I landed in this sweltering, trouble-strewn place, but now I really couldn't see a thing. I had made a false move, taken a step and found myself falling. Like Alice down the rabbit hole. There was no white rabbit down here though (or a talking donkey), and no hall full of doors. I heard a cough and a groan. Then a sigh.

'Can it get any worse?' I heard a high, rasping voice say.

'Who's that?' I hissed.

'One who's tired of affliction.'

'What?'

Another sigh, another groan.

'Are you condemned too?' the voice asked.

I tried to straighten myself up and realised my legs were entangled with someone else's. I could feel something oozing between my fingers as I pushed against the sludgy ground.

'Sorry,' I said.

'For what?'

'My legs, wrapped round yours.'

'Not mine. This is a big well, my condemned friend.'

'You mean... ugh!'

I recoiled and snatched my legs away from the other body. This time I did collide with the one speaking.

'Oof!' he groaned and spluttered, 'Is there no end to my suffering?'

'Who are you?'

I reached out to steady myself and found my fingers tangling in a beard. I flinched and recoiled again.

'Tell me that was *your* beard. Not some long dead facial fuzz.'

He laughed and I felt a hand pat my shoulder.

'You're all right,' he said, in that squeaky voice of his. 'Well you're not. We're two condemned men in a well, lying beside a rotting corpse. The future does not look like an undiscovered country. Oh I'm weary of this existence, I'm ready for death. Don't volunteer to be a prophet, it's the best way to lose friends and alienate people.'

I sat there in silence for a few minutes, mentally trying to figure a list of possible prophets.

'I never married you know,' he said after a while, 'I wanted to, I really wanted to, I was in love with a fine woman, we would have made a good team.'

'She er… dumped you?' I said, not putting too fine a point on it.

'Huh, if only. Would have made it easier. Like I say, don't be a prophet. You alienate people. I couldn't marry, wasn't allowed. Had to be a walking message to folks. By the way – this city's doomed. Don't settle here, don't have a family, don't plan for the future.' A pause. 'Don't marry.' Another pause. 'Sometimes it's like that you know. Being a prophet. Not so much what you say, as what you do. So I listened to the voice of God, whispering away, nudging me for weeks and eventually I gave in. Told her and broke her heart. Broke both our hearts.'

'That's terrible.'

'Maybe that's the case where you come from, but here God is in everything. And his presence doesn't always mean getting what you want. I told you, don't be a prophet. Costs you the earth.'

He sighed again. 'Since then I've done the lot. Spent my money on a piece of land when everyone else was selling up. Bought expensive pottery and smashed it in front of the government. Walked around in rotting underwear, looking the worst of fools. All to try and wake people up to the ways of God.'

'Did they listen?'

He laughed, and that set him off coughing for a while.

'Why do you think I'm in this well? They don't want to hear it. They want their news to be good. They don't want to change. They don't want to wake up and face the other way. They want a nice wide road and luxurious cart to take them along it. They hope that when I've rotted away down here all the bad news will dissipate with me. Then they can carry on with their lives and forget. Everyone doing what they consider right in their own eyes. Fools.' He spat in the dark. 'I'm trying to rescue them from the inevitable. If they go on living in their self-absorbed existence, plundering and gorging and ignoring the better way then destruction will come. Bound to. Death in the shape of invaders and marauders and raiders. The city's already long been under siege. It'll be captured soon. Won't just be you and I starving to death down here. Everyone's doomed. They brought it on themselves. Death and more death. But that's enough good news, what about you? Why they throw you down here?'

'They didn't. I'm searching for my friend Aladdin Strike.'

'In a sludge-strewn cistern?'

I pulled my legs up off the ground and hugged them to my chest, they were thick with coagulated grime and muck. The smell was foul. Absolutely appalling.

'I fell,' I said.

He sniffed. 'Well maybe you found him. Maybe that's him. The other character over there.'

I was about to say I doubted it, Aladdin wouldn't be caught dead in a place like this. But then perhaps that was just what had happened. He fell and broke his neck. The prophet under the palm tree had joked about him dying. Maybe it had really happened.

'You have a torch here?' I asked. 'A lamp?'

'If I had a lamp, my condemned friend, I would have lit it long ago.'

I was getting a little concerned about the 'condemned friend' reference.

'Is there a way out?'

'Of a well? The point of a well is that it gathers water, rather than leaking it.'

I ran my hands around the cold damp walls. Large insects crawled across my fingers. I swore one or two threw in a bite as they went.

'Underwear?' I said suddenly.

No response from the other guy.

'You said you went out in disintegrating underwear.'

'I said rotting – but you're right, it was disintegrating. I'd buried it by the river for a while, waited for the worms and the damp to have a go. Then I put it on and swanned around town, waiting for comments.'

I laughed. 'If you did that where I come from, no one would bat an eyelid. You'd probably have a designer company ringing you up wanting to franchise the look.'

'Well people noticed round here. So when they asked, I told them. Just like the river rotted these pants – God'll rot the pride and arrogance of the people here. They refuse to take note of his ways and his presence. Pleasing themselves and honouring idols. Oh, they laughed at me, most of them. But I bet when they put their underwear on every morning now they remember my mildewed pants. And maybe some of them are looking to their Maker as a result.'

We sat in silence for a while and then he started to sing. A brutally honest hymn about his struggles to do the right thing for his God. The tune was sombre, but catchy, a dirge that stuck in your head and played on a loop.

Something hit me. The hard end of a rope. Smacked me just above my right eye. I lashed out in the darkness and found it dangling there. There was something tied to it. Rags and old clothes.

'Hey!' a voice called from somewhere above us. 'Make a harness with the rags and we'll pull you out.'

'God be praised,' said the prophet. 'They've had a change of heart up there. Quick, before they change again. They can be fickle round here. You go first. Come on.'

He helped tie the rags together in the dark and he shoved them under my armpits as a kind of hoist. We hollered back up the well and I felt the rope tighten.

Pretty soon I was on my way back to fresh air and daylight. Well, fresh air and night. Firm hands gripped me as I neared the top and they hauled me back up over the edge. I found myself dumped at the feet of a gang of soldiers. They looked bewildered.

'Who are you?' one of them demanded.

'It's all right,' I told them, 'I fell down there by mistake. The prophet's coming up next. Throw the rope back down.'

The soldiers looked towards a sharply dressed official, he nodded and they dropped the rope and harness back into the dark. They turned from me and gathered around the top of the well. I took my chance and slipped away while their attention was diverted.

12. The Woman in White

I looked around in the semi-darkness, I was in a courtyard, torches lit the pathway out of there. I went. I didn't fancy taking my chances back outside among the besieging army so I looked for the nearest nook to rest my head for a while.

I found a broken door hanging off its hinges. Inside there was straw and a water trough but nothing else. That would do for me. I snuck in and bedded down. The straw smelt of animals but I didn't care. I was soon dead to the world.

I'm lying by the road, off my head after another night out, as ever abandoned by my so-called friends, and yes, here we go again, I grab at my pockets and discover the scabs have run off with my cash. My wallet's here but never more empty. They'll laugh about it tomorrow as we shift stuff in the factory, but it's no joke to me. Happens too often. Me left nursing the old headache and short of cash to see me through the week yet again. I hear a step and know that for once one of them has come back for me, maybe to help me up, maybe to apologise, maybe to give me at least my bus fare home. But the hand reaching for me doesn't go for my arm, it goes for my face instead. Slapping me hard, and again. A third time and I'm seeing stars. I feel a boot in my ribs and smell urine and mud on the leather. I tuck my head under my arms and hug the floor as the fists rain down on me. In my head I go somewhere else, a safe place, another

world where these things don't happen. But the beating and the spitting and the cursing goes on.
On.
And on.
And on.

I awoke with a start and sat up, my forehead was a film of sweat. I wiped at it. My breathing was coming thick and fast. I went to the trough, there was a metal scoop hanging off it by a leather strap. I took it and drank the water. It was fresh enough. I caught sight of a leather flask by the side of the trough, I took that and filled it up. No good. There was a hole in the bottom and it leaked rapidly. I sat back in the straw and caught my breath. That dream. That same dream. It came back again and again. Just when I thought I was done with it. Maybe this was all a dream, the sandwich maker and Aladdin and the green smoking drink. I couldn't tell anymore, I was losing all sense of reality. Talking donkeys and prophets down wells – it was all doing my head in. Enough was enough. I lay back down again, hoping to sleep again and wake up in reality. I'd be happy with that nondescript existence now.

I fell into a restless world of tossing and turning and dreaming about donkeys reciting long sections of *War and Peace*. This turned into a musical and a whole choir of mules appeared and broke into a number about Mr Darcy. On unicycles. Juggling pairs of mouldy pants and balancing e-readers on their heads as they pedalled along.

I opened my eyes and my head immediately had that thick-headed fug about it, the type of thing you get from sleeping but not resting. It was daylight and the first thing I noticed was the woman in white sitting on the edge of the water trough. There was something familiar about her. She had short black hair, a round face and rosy cheeks. The well on the mountain flashed through my mind. The well and the bucket.

'You should eat something,' she said, 'you'll need it for your journey. Elijah got depressed when he didn't eat.'

I sat up, clapped a hand on the top of my head and tried to shake myself free of the fug. It didn't work.

'Elijah?' I said, my mouth clammy and my throat dry.

'Sounds like you need a drink too,' she held out the flask towards me. A little water slopped from the mouthpiece.

'That thing leaks,' I said, with a dismissive wave of my hand. 'I tried it last night.'

'Really?' she said.

I looked again. It wasn't leaking.

'Odd, I tried filling that last night.'

'Oh well, things often look different in the daylight. Here.' She handed me the flask along with a bulky leather pouch. It was stuffed full of fruit and bread.

'Eat!' she said, jabbing a finger towards the bundle.

'Oh, and a quick wash in here might not be a bad idea.'

She stood and indicated the trough with her thumb.

'Don't suppose you've got any shower gel?' I said. '*Lynx*... maybe?'

She laughed. 'You're a few thousand years ahead of yourself, mate. Water'll do for now.'

I stuck my head in the trough and doused my head and shoulders. When I came up for air she was turning to leave.

'How do I get out of here?' I said. 'D'you know? I mean, the siege and all? It's dangerous.'

'Do what the donkey told you,' she said.

'How d'you know about the donkey? Was he for real?'

'I know because we sent him. We do that sort of thing. And yes he was for real.'

'He didn't tell me how to get out.'

She scratched her head and flicked her hair from her eyes. 'Oh. He's such an airhead. He's always forgetting vital bits of the message. Okay.' And she walked outside.

'What d'you mean – okay?' I ran to the broken door and looked out. I was hit by the sudden bustle from the street, bodies and the muddle of harried chatter, but there was no sign of the woman in white. People hurried up and down, many of them clutching children and belongings. There were crowds of them looking for somewhere to hide, the noise was overwhelming, but the woman in white had vanished.

13. Joseph

I went back inside, sat down on the straw and opened the food pouch. I wolfed down a couple of figs and an apple. I scrutinised the flask. No leaks. None whatsoever. I found myself wondering whether it might refill itself when I'd had a drink. It didn't. Still – no leaks. That was an improvement. Then I heard the lips flapping. It was him. I swear he was almost smiling.

'Come on,' he said, twitching his ears, 'I've been sent to get you out of here.'

'Really? You mean… you're telling me that woman in white…'

'Hey, she ain't no woman,' he said. 'And for the record she ain't no man either. Come on. This place is getting desperate, I need to get out of here before someone tries to cook me in a red wine sauce. Plus I want to get back and finish *Murder on the Orient Express*. I'm about three pages away from finding out whodunnit.'

I opened my mouth to reply but he held up a hoof.

'Don't spoil the end for me, or I won't get you out of here. Now come on.'

Once again the creature cut a swift path, ducking and diving, dodging people and obstacles. I did my best to keep up, nearly dropping my food parcel on the way. He screeched to a halt in front of a doorway.

'I apologise about this now, but it's for your own

good.'

'Apologise for what?'

'This,' he said and he kicked open the door. 'Travelling mercies,' he said, 'you might well need them.' And he nodded towards the inside.

I went in. It was a latrine. And the cleaning staff were clearly on holiday or strike.

'You're kidding me,' I said out loud.

There was no reply. I looked back. The donkey had fled. I looked back at the foul smelling, randomly streaked water closet. It could have been worse. I'm not sure how, but I told myself that to keep me going.

I stuffed the food and water under my shirt and inside my belt for safekeeping, then, like Renton in *Trainspotting*, Roddy in *Flushed Away* and Andy in *Shawshank* I stuck my head down the toilet. I couldn't imagine my shoulders getting through the mouth of the pipe but somehow they did. Either my body contorted or this was a world where cistern plumbing could adjust as necessary. I pushed on, ignoring the detritus that came my way, and keeping my mouth firmly shut. Every so often I felt warm, soft missiles bumping my cheeks and lips. I pressed on. I'm sure this lavatory system was ahead of its time for it looked way too modern, but I wasn't arguing (I wouldn't have dared open my mouth) and eventually, my hair matted and my face smeared, I crawled out into daylight beyond the city walls. I immediately heard a shout and thought the donkey had sold me out. I didn't look back, just scrambled up and ran. More voices joined in the calling but I wasn't risking a look. I had to get away from the city as fast as possible.

They were catching up with me. I could hear their threats and curses getting louder now. I spotted a well, it was a desperate ploy but I couldn't keep going. I sat on the edge, swung my legs inside and lowered myself in, placing my feet on a couple of indents in the wall below. I clung onto the top for dear life and pressed my body hard against the pitted wall as I heard them approaching. They were talking hurriedly, must have been at least half a dozen up there. The voices stopped and there was silence for a while. I'd got away with it. I let out a sigh of relief. Then the face appeared, grinning at me over the edge.

'You don't want to hang around in there,' the man said and without any warning he grabbed my wrists and hauled me up.

There were ten of them. An obvious family resemblance suggested brothers.

'You gonna kill me now?' I said, backing away.

'No, but if you keep going you'll be back in that well again.'

They laughed, and it wasn't mockery, just good natured. One of them held out his hand. He had long brown hair, strong, handsome features, and a dimple right there in the centre of his chin. 'I'm Reuben, these are my brothers. What are you doing round here?'

'I was running from the siege.'

'What siege?'

'In the city.'

'What city?'

I pointed back the way I had come. We all turned to look. There was no sign of any city on the horizon. No soldiers either.

'You had a blow on the head or something?' one of the other brothers said.

'No, but I have seen some strange things round here.'

The others laughed.

'Probably something you ate,' said Reuben.

'Hey,' said the other brother, a guy with similar features but shorter, 'You ain't got any food have you?'

I pulled out the bundle. It was still fairly full but nowhere near enough for these growing lads.

'Shame, we're starving.'

'Simeon, leave him. I'm sure one of the men'll be along soon with food from dad.'

'Talk of the devil,' said one of the others, and he pointed into the distance.

A lone figure was walking towards them.

'Oh great,' said Simeon.

'Well, you wanted food,' said Reuben.

'Yes, but I didn't want him.'

We watched the young figure approach through the shimmering heat. He had the same facial features as the others, and a coat worth dying for. He also had a shoulder bag stuffed with bottles and parcels.

'Hey Joe,' said Reuben, 'good to see you.'

But the tone of his voice didn't say that, it said something else.

Joe gave them all a huge smile. 'I brought you lunch,' he said and he handed over the bag.

'Had any dreams on the way?' Simeon asked and the others laughed, this time there was mockery in the laughter.

'No but I had some more ideas.'

'Leave it Joe, we're tired,' said Reuben.

'Who's this?' asked the younger brother, holding out his hand to me.

'We found him in a well,' said Simeon. 'He said he's running from a siege.'

Joe frowned and scanned the horizon. 'You must have come a long way,' he said.

'Oh yes,' I muttered, 'I've come an awful long way.'

'Ever have any dreams?' Joe asked.

I looked away. 'Yea, but I don't remember them.'

'Shame, I like dreams.'

'Yea but we don't,' muttered Simeon. 'Not yours anyway. Always on about everybody bowing down.'

'Not my fault if I dream that.'

'Shut it Joe.'

The brothers were tucking into the food and making short work of it. Joe stepped away from them and sat down on his own.

'We gotta do something about him,' said Simeon.

'Yea,' said one of the others.

I didn't like the tone of their voices so I left them and went to sit next to Joe. I offered him food from my bundle as he didn't seem to have any of his own. He took a hunk of bread.

'I get these dreams at night,' he said. 'I think they mean something but no one else does.'

I had a flashback to a childhood bedtime book about Egypt. Something about sheaves of corn and stars bowing down.

'They do mean something,' I said, 'believe me. I know.'

'How d'you know?' he looked at me sharply, a crumb of bread in the corner of his mouth.

'I'm not sure.' I was startling myself with my sudden level of conviction, 'I guess I know because… well, I come from somewhere else and… we've heard of you.'

He grinned and jumped up. 'Really! No way!'

I nodded. 'I'd better not say too much, but hang on to your dreams, even if everything seems lost.'

'Why not? Why can't you say too much? Tell me.'

It was an odd moment. All I could think about was *Back to the Future* and the danger of messing with the space-time continuum. Changing the past by messing with the present. I just shrugged. It was easier than explaining. Joe turned and ran back to his brothers.

'Guess what? I'm famous,' he yelled at them.

Simeon rolled his eyes.

'We don't care,' one of the other brothers said.

'You should,' said Joe, his eyes wide.

Simeon stood up, along with one or two of the others.

'No we should not. In fact, I think you need a lesson in humility and manners.'

'That would be two lessons wouldn't it?' he said. 'Humility and manners.'

'Don't be smart, Joe, you're pushing us now.'

Joe backed away as a group of them made a move towards him. Suddenly Simeon lunged and grabbed him. I leapt up.

'Hey!' I said.

'Keep out of this. It's not your business,' said Reuben.

I hesitated, this was one of those 'get involved or ignore it' moments.

'Please, it was my fault,' I said stepping towards them. 'I told him he was famous.'

One of the brothers shoved me away. His craggy fist slammed hard against my chest as he pushed me. Simeon turned his back on me.

'Let's kill him,' he hissed.

For moment I thought he was talking about me and I couldn't believe how my luck had changed again, then the truth dawned and I froze.

'We don't want his blood on our hands,' Reuben said, 'that would be stupid.'

'Who would know? We can tell dad a wild animal savaged him. Take that stupid coat of his and rip it to shreds as if he was attacked. That would really make my day. Kill Joe and slaughter his coat.'

'No!' Reuben stepped in, he clearly had the authority here. He took Joe by the arm. 'I agree we should do something. Punish him. But not that.'

Joe's eyes were wide with alarm, his lips were moving but I couldn't catch what he was saying, some kind of pleading perhaps. The rest of the brothers were clearly bent on some sort of revenge. They were sneering at Joe and making snide comments to one another.

Reuben looked back at the well, the one they'd pulled me from. 'Let's throw him in there,' he said. 'That way if he dies, he dies. Nothing to do with us. Let nature take its course.'

Joe looked at me, his eyes telegraphing a plea for help. I made a move but Reuben held up his hand.

'This is not your affair,' he said. 'Go on your way.'

I looked back at Joe, he was terrified. Simeon clenched his fists and moved towards me. There and then I made a backup plan in my head and nodded. I turned and walked away.

'No,' yelled Joe.

I heard them dragging him towards the well. I would be back, and I would set him free. It would be stupid to argue with them all now, the odds were all wrong. But later, alone, I could rescue him. Maybe that's what Reuben was hoping for anyway. That his brother would somehow be found and freed when they had gone. Reuben didn't seem the killing kind to me. Whatever that meant.

I walked on for an age. Time passed slowly. At one point I passed a group of traders, but I kept my distance. Eventually, after hiding in a clump of rocks for an hour or two I turned and went back. The brothers were gone. I crept up to the well and crouched over it.

'Joe!' I called.

Nothing. I called again. Still no reply. The well was empty. Then I remembered the bedtime book again. I was too late. Joe would be on his way to Egypt now, dragged along by that group of traders. I had a strange feeling, like I'd failed, but I knew Joseph wouldn't. He just had years of waiting ahead of him. I couldn't really have done much about that? To intervene would surely have created problems. I turned away from the well and spotted the dark stain on the ground. At least one of the brothers' wishes had come true. They'd trashed the coat they hated so much. Dipped it in blood so they could spin their lost-brother sob story for their father back at home.

14. Rahab

Exhausted from my bad night and the events of the previous day I curled up in the clump of rocks again and fell asleep for a while. Strange things happened while I slept. Fortunately, not that fearful dream again. But when I awoke it was dark and I was lying outside another city, right at the foot of the wall. Whether someone had lifted me and dumped me there, or whether the ground had opened up and produced this place I had no idea. Perhaps the talking donkey had given me a lift. Maybe the woman in white had conjured the place. Anything seemed possible round here. I heard a scratching sound above me and looked up to see pale fingers protruding from the wall, working to secure a red rope from a window.

A face appeared, looked straight at me and then withdrew quickly. Feet appeared, followed by legs and the body of a man. I rolled to my right and pressed myself hard against the wall. It was no hiding place and I was quite obviously visible when the man descended the rope and dropped near enough to kill me. He didn't though, he took one look at me, looked startled, then waved to another set of feet in the window above. A second figure dropped and landed beside the first. They both stared at me, put fingers to their lips and then turned and crept hastily away. The second one tripped and sprawled, then looked back at me, clambered up and hurried on. I looked back up at the window, and saw the same face I had first spotted looking down at me. I shrugged and put my hands together in a pleading gesture. She stared at me then with a quick flick of her head indicated I come up. I grabbed the red rope and somehow hauled myself up. In reality I doubt I'd ever climb a rope like that, but nothing about this world was surprising me anymore. I scuffed my way up to the window and the woman grabbed me and hauled me in.

'Are you another?' she snapped at me.

I looked into her eyes, they were hazel, narrow and heavily made-up.

'Another what?'

'Spy!' she hissed.

I shook my head, various images of James Bond suddenly crowding my imagination.

'You mean, like those two?' I said, indicating the window with my thumb.

She nodded furiously. 'Yes! Who else?' Then she stood back a little and a smile crept across her bright lips. 'Oh,' she said, as if suddenly realising. 'You're just a customer. Very clever.'

Spy? Customer? I didn't get it.

'Sneaking in on the back of those two, very shrewd. But I'm afraid you're too late. Come back tomorrow.'

'I just need a place to sleep till it's light.'

'Really? Nothing else?'

I shook my head.

'You can pay?'

I shook my head again. Then I stopped and held up my hand. 'Wait a minute.'

I hunted in my pockets, pulled out a fistful of strange coins I'd never seen before. She slapped her hands on her hips. 'Can't pay eh?' she said.

'I er… I forgot.'

She looked at the coins. 'It'll cost you. Sleeping with me is more expensive than staying awake.'

It took me a while to work that out, and while I was chewing on it she helped herself to four coins. It meant nothing to me, I hadn't even had the money when I went to sleep.

'You can have the roof, where the spies were, it's only a few hours to daylight now. You go up and I'll see you in the morning. I'm tired. It's been a hard night.'

I clambered up and lay down. Sleep came and went but I snatched enough of it to make the darkness pass soon enough. She appeared with food, some soap and a bowl of water.

'Breakfast,' she said, 'and you should wash.'

I hadn't taken the advice of the woman in white, just a quick splash in that trough, so I guess I smelt worse than ever. At least this time I had been given soap too. This woman, on the other hand, smelt great.

'I have work to do, so you need to be out of here soon,' she said.

I remembered something that had crossed my mind as I lay down to sleep.

'The red rope, you should make sure you take it down,' I said.

She shook her head. 'It's my lifeline. Literally,' she said.

I tore at the bread and wedged a piece between my teeth. 'Why?'

'Those spies weren't customers last night. They were Israelites come to check out the city before they attack us. The word on the street is that they'll soon take this place. I made the spies promise to spare me and my family. They told me to leave the red rope as a marker and they'd make sure I wasn't harmed. I'm not taking it down. No way.' She took a sliver of my bread and bit on it. 'People are terrified you know. You must have heard.'

I shook my head. 'I'm not from round here,' I said.

'You're lucky,' she said. She picked at the bread with her painted nails and put tiny lumps of it between her lips. 'They'll kill us all won't they? People say they're brutal.'

'I'm not so sure. Don't believe everything you hear, bad news never needs fertiliser. It grows and bears plenty of bad fruit without much help.'

She frowned and shrugged. 'I think my life will be over soon. What's a prostitute worth to anyone? I mean, really – in the grand scheme of things. Why should they spare my life?'

'Everyone's life is worth something,' I said, but I could hear the lack of conviction in my own voice as I said it. I believed it at that moment, I really did, but I could recall plenty of times when I had doubted it.

'I don't do it out of choice you know. The job, I mean. No prostitute ever would. I need to live. Sometimes I hate myself and I can't see a way out. If you offered me a new life tomorrow I'd take it.' She snapped her fingers. 'Just like that.'

'Well, maybe those spies are offering you that,' I said.

She thought for a moment. 'Maybe. We'll see.'

We sat in the morning light, chewing bread and dates and watching the sun's rays playing over the new day. The hills rose beyond the city walls and I spotted a couple of distant figures moving over the crest.

'D'you think that's them? Over there – the spies?' I said pointing them out to her.

We watched the little creatures weaving over the rocky ground. She ummed and ahhed.

'D'you think they'll attack today?' I asked.

She shook her head, her tattooed hand twisting her auburn hair in her fingers.

'They said it'll be three days. They have to go look around then go back and make a report. But they'll come. I know they will.'

We watched them for a while till the silence was broken by a couple of heavy-handed thuds from below.

'Your customer?' I said, but she looked worried.

'No. Too early. And I don't recognise that sound,

my man doesn't announce himself with such a crass beating. We have a code.' She listened.

The thuds came again, three this time.

'It's the king's men,' she said, 'must be. They came looking for the spies last night. I lied, told them they'd already left for the hill country. I could be in trouble.'

She stood up but I grabbed her arm.

'Then let's get out of here, escape till the heat dies down,' I said.

She gave me a strange look. 'And go where?'

'I don't know, somewhere quiet.'

'What about my customer?'

'Leave a message, postpone till tomorrow.'

The thuds sounded again, and there were voices this time too. Making thundering demands.

'It is them,' she said. 'No doubt about it.'

'Right, let's go then.'

I hastily threw cold water over my face then clambered off the roof and back to the red-roped window. She meanwhile scribbled a coded message on a piece of parchment which she left by her bed. I helped her out of the window. We slipped down the rope and ran for some rough ground. We fell behind a rock and she burst out laughing.

'This is ridiculous,' she said.

'You don't know the half of it,' I said.

We sat back against the rock and caught our breath.

'When did you last do this?' I said. 'Go out with a strange man?'

'I spend every night with strange men,' she said.

'Yes, but not like this. Come on, let's find a quiet place.'

We found a forest and walked for a while. We told each other our names and a few faltering stories. I managed to squeeze bits of information from her. It wasn't easy, she seemed a very private person. We were well suited.

'There's a popular story where I come from,' I told her, 'we call it *Pretty Woman*.'

She stopped and eyed me closely. 'Is that flattery? Are you trying to start something?' she said.

'No. Listen. It's about a businessman who picks up a prostitute and then falls in love with her.'

'You are trying to start something.'

'I'm not a businessman, and anyway, anything like that would be very… unworkable.'

'So you don't like me?'

It was such a loaded question. How could I ever answer that and come out unscathed?

'Of course I do. Look at us, we're practically on a date right now.'

Wrong answer. She didn't like that.

'You can just pay me you know,' she said. 'If that's what you want. It's cheaper than just sleeping on my roof.'

I laughed, though I'm not sure I was supposed to. 'What I'm saying is this, maybe, in your new life with the Israelites you'll meet a "businessman",' I made the quotation marks with my fingers, 'and you'll fall in love and have a new start. And maybe you'll have a son who'll... be part of a royal dynasty.' I shook my head as the thoughts crowded one another out. 'No – more than that, an everlasting royal line.'

It sounded preposterous and she didn't like it. I could see that. I hadn't intended to spill any of this, but the story had come from somewhere deep down and I was sure there was truth in it.

'Why are you making all this up?' she said, her face colouring. 'Why are you saying all this? Are you mocking me? Is that it? Or what? Are you trying to seduce me, to get something from me? I told you, just pay me.' She sounded irritable now.

'No. It's not that. Look, I do know that I'm not your "Mr Right", your "businessman",' more finger-formed quotation marks, 'that's way too complicated.' Even as I said this I felt my heart sinking, I wasn't expecting that. I hesitated for a moment.

She looked at me, threw up her hands impatiently. 'Yes?' she said. 'And?'

'Just... just trust me. When the Israelites take Jericho, you'll be okay.'

'So... what? Are you a prophet?'

'No! I've met a few of those recently and I'm dead sure I'm not.'

'Yet here you are predicting my future.'

I took a few steps in silence. I didn't want to care and I hadn't realised I knew so much about her. I hadn't realised I'd retained so much biblical information from my youth. The names of Rahab and Boaz, Naomi and Ruth were chasing one another in my head. I suddenly remembered a picture from one of my childhood books. A piece of cartoon art about Jesus' family tree. They were all on there, those names. All linked and paving the way for the Messiah. I had clearly taken in more than I realised when I had been making paper aeroplanes and chewing gum in the back row. The realisation stunned me a little.

'What?' she said, as I stood there staring at her. 'What are you thinking?'

I shook my head. It was all too complicated. Where had all those insights come from? Maybe she was right. Perhaps I was a prophet, of sorts. I let the topic drop. We walked on for a while in silence. The mood lifted and she chatted about other things.

'When I was little I had dreams of being a princess,' she said. 'Big palace. Servants. Beautiful clothes. I've come close you know.' And she gave me a wry smile. 'One or two of my clients come from royal stock.' She laughed. 'That's close isn't it? Princess for twenty minutes or so?'

I didn't like that. I was starting to feel protective towards her.

'Here look,' she said, 'a stream! You can wash properly. At last. You really need to wash.'

I was fed up. This world was full of women telling

me to wash.

'Give me a break,' I snapped, 'I climbed through a sewer. I was desperate, it was that or death.'

'Brave man,' she said, 'come on.'

She grabbed my shirt and peeled it off. The stream ran across the path, she knelt and buried my shirt in water. 'Better do your other clothes too,' she said.

I looked around, feeling ridiculously self-conscious.

'Come on,' she said, 'I'm helping you, and I've seen everything in my job believe me.'

I wished she hadn't said that. It made me feel small and frustrated. And angry about all those men. All those uncaring nightly visitors. I snuck behind a bush and threw her my jeans. While she was rinsing them I went further downstream and gave myself a decent dousing. When I looked up, my hair streaming and eyes full of water, she was there looking at me. How long she'd been there I do not know. She just smiled and threw me my jeans. I dragged them on, still soaking wet.

'You should dry your shirt for a while,' she said, 'put it on a tree. It won't take long.'

She hung it up but I was hit by this sudden feeling of exposure. I felt a fool. I went over and grabbed the shirt, snagging it on a branch as I pulled it down. I shoved myself back inside it.

'What's wrong?' she asked.

'Nothing. I... nothing.'

'You're embarrassed now, aren't you? About being with me. There's no one here to see. And anyway I have top clients, believe me. That's why the king came looking for the spies in my house. They know me. They're not ashamed of me.'

'I'm not ashamed of you,' I blustered. 'I'm… I'm...'

Of course, it was the opposite. Right then, standing there in those pathetic, damp clothes I wanted to be a hero and take her away from all this. I wanted to be strong and romantic and whisk her off her feet and give her the new life she wanted. I also found her beautiful and mysterious and irresistible. And I fancied the hell out of her. All kinds of desires were doing battle in my brain. She was talking but I didn't hear a word. Couldn't hear anything because I was just looking at her, pretending to be interested but actually too busy studying her face, her eyes, her mouth, her expression. I wanted to make it all right for her, but I couldn't. I couldn't change anything. And that made everything seem wrong. I needed to get out of there but didn't want to leave her. I tore my gaze away and slumped onto a rock, squeezing water from the hem of my shirt. I kept working at that for a while, saying nothing. There were no words useful enough. I knew she was looking at me, willing me to look back at her, but I wasn't having any of it.

After a while she said, 'I get it. I see now.' And that was all. She turned and began to walk slowly back towards her life in the city. And I'll never know what it was she figured she'd got, what it was she thought she saw. I'd love to tell you this is one of those stories where two people get separated by circumstance but then meet five years later and get it on forever. But I can't. All I can say is I watched her walk away, hoping she'd look back. But she never did, and in the end I turned and walked the other way and kept going until I met a stranger pacing up and down by a couple of stone pillars covered in carvings. I was glad of the distraction, glad of so many of the distractions that followed. The adventures that unfolded weren't easy, but then life never is. But dealing with the troubles and difficulties weaned me off her.

15. Ehud

He looked at me as if he'd known me forever. As if we were drinking buddies or snooker pals.

'Come on,' he said, 'you're late.'

I looked around to see if he meant someone else. We were alone. My clothes were still damp and I must have looked a mess.

'Me? I'm late?' I said.

'Yea, if we're going to do this we have to do it properly. And we don't have much time. Look.'

He flicked open the right side of his robe. There was a short handled knife strapped to his thigh.

'I don't have one of those,' I said and he laughed.

'Course you don't,' he said. 'I made this myself. Specially for the job. I hope you're not armed at all, are you?'

I shook my head.

'Good, because they'll search us when we go back in and I don't want them finding anything on you and refusing us entry. I sent the others away so that we can keep this simple.'

'The others?'

He sighed and checked the strap on his knife.

'Yes, the others. You remember, the guys sent with me to carry the king's taxes. The money's delivered and they've gone back thinking that's the end of it now. But, as we discussed, you and I are going back to make the special delivery.'

'The special delivery?'

'Yes, the special delivery. Now remember, leave the talking to me, anybody asks, you're just there as a trainee. Okay? Now, we'll both go in and I'll tell them what we agreed. Then when we get inside the royal chamber you stand back and I'll move close. He's bound to fall for it, his ego is as big as his gut. Okay? Got it?'

I'd got nothing but this tall muscular guy didn't give me chance to say. He had scars on his neck and cheek and another long one down his arm. He'd obviously seen some action and been in some scrapes but his body looked jammed with power so he could clearly handle himself. He turned and started walking. I followed. As we left the carved stones behind we quickly took up on a road towards a royal palace, the place was clearly dripping with opulence and wealth. Two guards barred our way at the gate.

'I am Ehud, the king's messenger. I brought the taxes to him earlier today and now I have a message for his majesty.'

The guards looked at one another.

'An *important* message,' Ehud emphasised.

'Arms out, legs akimbo,' said the taller guard, he came close and I could smell his last meal on his breath.

He patted us down and checked the inside of our left legs for hidden weapons. Just the place where a right-handed man hides his knife for killing a king.

He was fascinated by my 21st century pockets but disappointed by the lack of military hardware in any of them. He stepped back and the shorter of the two nodded and led us through the gates, and down a myriad of corridors and archways.

'Can you remember your way out of here?' I leant in and whispered to Ehud.

He grimaced and pushed me away, indicating that I shut up.

Two golden doors about 15 feet high swung open and I got my first sight of his majesty. A huge figure in a purple robe surrounded by servants, slaves and concubines. He took one look at us and shooed the women, and the workers moved a little further away. His hand was studded with rings and coated in grape juice and sweat. The floor in front of him was tiled in black and white and a group of slaves appeared to be taking part in a life-size game of chess.

'Knight to queen four,' the king said and his voice came out like a coarse rumble, like gravel in a cement mixer.

A slave in a leather horse's head made the move and collided with a buxom queen. She squealed and keeled over. Everyone applauded, the women, the slaves, even the pieces on both sides of the board. I got the feeling his majesty couldn't lose.

'Congratulations your majesty,' said Ehud, stepping forward and bowing.

I considered doing the same but he must have read

my mind and he indicated I stay back with the flat of his hand. So I just bowed where I was.

'Not more taxes,' said the gravelly voice. 'I haven't spent the last lot yet.'

And all those who had just applauded laughed with suitable vigour. Ehud forced a smile.

'No your majesty, I bring a message this time. One worth more than gold.'

The king's bulky face frowned, his cheeks wobbling and his fleshy forehead rippling with furrows. A few beads of sweat dripped from him and a nearby slave moved forward and caught them in a gold goblet. He looked at us for a long time. No one said anything, then the gravelly voice rumbled again.

'Castle to king's bishop three.'

A slave wearing a silver brick-shaped crown took three steps and everyone applauded again. It was not clear who his majesty was playing but there was no doubt who was going to win.

He extended a short stubby finger and beckoned.

'Come, tell me then.'

It was Ehud's turn to grimace.

'I... we... need to be alone with you, your majesty. This message comes from the highest source.'

'The highest source?'

Ehud nodded. The king looked to me for confirmation and I nodded too.

'Very well,' he shooed the entourage away and a chief slave guided them out of the huge doors. When the doors had closed with an almighty, floor shaking crash the king beckoned us closer. We were now alone with him.

'The highest source, you say?' he said.

We crossed the chessboard tiles. The buxom queen's crown lay discarded on the floor. I stepped over it.

'King Eglon,' Ehud began, 'this message… is from God.'

The king rose up from his throne and leant towards the two of us. Ehud wasted no time in flicking his robe aside, grabbing the sword and shoving it hard into Eglon's ample gut. The king groaned a gravelly groan and Ehud pushed harder on the sword. Eglon fell back and his stomach slid open. Pink and grey slime oozed out, lubricated by an awful lot of blood. Ehud's hand was hidden in the rolls of fat, he had pushed the sword so far in. He left the weapon where it was and stepped back to avoid the gory torrent. The stench filled the room. Ehud wiped red sludge from his fingers on the king's fine robe.

I clapped a hand to my face.

'He's soiled himself,' Ehud said, but he didn't seem bothered by the smell.

'Does it have to be this way?' I said, 'couldn't you just vote him out?'

'Vote? What's that?' He jabbed a finger at Eglon, there were still red smears around the fingernail. 'This monster has been around long enough. He had every chance to be a great leader but you can see the kind of man he was. In it for himself. For 18 years this Moabite slug has dominated us, ripping the heart and soul from the nation with his crippling taxes and evil ways. Enough now. The rich fool must die. Time for some justice.'

There was a knock on the great doors. Ehud put a finger to his lips and beckoned me to follow him. He slipped out of a side door into a smaller vestibule. A.k.a. the king's toilet. The place was awash with silk hangings and detailed mosaics. Soaps and lotions of all shapes and colours lined the side of the huge, oval bath. Ehud pointed at the vast royal loo seat. It was solid gold.

'That's where we're going,' he said.

'You're kidding me,' I said.

'Kidding?'

'Joking.' Not another toilet dive, please.

'It's our only way. Be thankful it's the king's, it'll be cleaner than anyone else's.'

'True, and if that smell in there is anything to go by, I reckon he's not been in a while.'

So like Renton and Roddy and Andy we dived into the toilet bowl and squeezed our way down the pipe to freedom. Water of various shades flooded my eyes and nose, and bits of green, brown, grey and black sludge came at me, bounced off and no doubt left their mark. Once again the system looked way too modern to me, like a dream where your own reality collides with someone else's.

We emerged into the daylight, checked for danger and ran into the hills. We didn't dare look too closely at ourselves or each other, instead we made for the nearest water supply. It turned out to be a waterfall and the two of us flung ourselves, fully clothed, into the showering flow and tried our level best to wash away King Eglon's crap.

'So can I ask – what do you normally do?' I said, as we started wading back to shore.

'This.'

'Kill people?'

'It's the oldest solution in the world. Old as Cain and Abel. Plenty of work. I'm a busy man.'

'It's hardly a solution. If I remember rightly Cain was advised by God to resist bumping off his brother.'

Ehud shrugged and sat down on the bank.

'Where I come from this kind of thing is definitely frowned upon,' I said. 'Definitely.'

'You mean I'd be in a little trouble?'

'A *little* trouble? And the rest.'

'So no one kills anyone where you live? Not even for justice?'

'Well, yea they do, happens all the time. But... well, what I mean is... it's not viewed in this way.' This was more complicated than I'd expected.

'Look,' he said, 'You don't live here right? So you haven't suffered under Eglon. You haven't seen what it's done to your family and neighbours. To your country. Until you live with it, how can you make a judgement of it? When Jael took a tent peg and turned it into a murder weapon, she wasn't doing it for herself. It was about freedom and justice. You're privileged if you live in a place where you're not confronted with the need to choose violence as a way forward.'

Something was rattling in my brain, like a dog scratching at the door of my memory. I was back in Sunday school, grimacing in the back row as Miss read us a story about a violent camping incident.

'Wait a minute – you mentioned Jael, she tricked Sisera into sleeping in her tent and while he was out cold she skewered him through the temple – isn't that right?'

'Yes, because he was ruthless, he was oppressing the people. Had done for two decades.'

'But the Bible…'

'The Bible?'

'You know, the sacred writings, the stories we have, they tell us that the people rebelled against God, so he gave them over to these tyrants. Despots like Eglon and Sisera – the people brought the injustice on themselves because they ignored the good road, they discarded the ways of God. It's like… like…' I made mental grasps for some equivalent. I snapped my fingers. 'Where I come from everyone's terrified about the planet dying. But we brought the terror on ourselves because we treated the world badly. We forgot the good ways of God, rejected compassion and respect and that sort of thing.'

He looked at me, ran a hand over the jagged scar on his cheek, then down the one on his arm. The muscle rippled and stood out like the tread on a tractor tyre. He was a powerful man. He looked serious, I wondered if I'd overstepped the mark. Thank goodness he'd left his short-handled sword in Eglon's belly. Mind you, his hands alone had probably finished a few people. He sighed and stepped towards me, I pulled back a little.

'I don't have an answer for you,' he said quietly, which made it sound a little menacing. 'I just know what I have to do. Here, now, for these people. And I have to do it right now.' He stuck out his hand suddenly and I jumped a little. 'I have more killing to organise in the name of justice. We have to take advantage of the chaos that'll be erupting in the palace now. You want to join us and fight for freedom? You'd be welcome.'

Images of Eglon slumped on his throne, spilling his guts, flashed through my mind. I had no stomach for it. Not unlike Eglon. And as I thought again of his death I was suddenly back on that bridge. The future closing around me like a couple of dark, double doors, cold and impregnable. Clouding my mind and blocking any future I might have had. I shook my head. Partly to rid my mind of the memory and partly in reply to Ehud's invitation. Ehud nodded, he seemed to understand. He grabbed my hand and shook it, there was no doubt he had the most powerful grip in the world. Then he patted my shoulder and turned to go.

'One thing,' I said. 'How do you know me? When we met you acted like we were old friends?'

He laughed. 'How else was I going to immediately enlist your help? I don't know you at all. It's an old trick. If you need an accomplice bluff your way with the first likely candidate you see. What's your name by the way?'

I told him.

'You must be short of candidates,' I added, 'if I was the most likely.'

He narrowed his eyes then punched my shoulder. It hurt.

'You did fine.' he said.

'But you didn't need me.'

'Exactly. That's why you did fine. You were there if I did.'

And he went. Just like that. Walked away to round up an army and rout Eglon's men. As I watched him go I had the vague feeling that something about our conversation was adrift. The feeling nagged at me so I pulled out my moleskine notebook and put a scribble in it. As I wrote it hit me, though goodness knows how I knew. Ehud came before Jael in the book of Judges, we'd just discussed an incident that hadn't even happened yet. How did we both know about it? How? This bizarre odyssey was messing with everything. But maybe that was only to be expected when you drank green smoking liquid and stuck wires in yourself to invade the Good Book.

16. Sarah

I left the waterfall and trekked on through the hills. I was no nearer to finding Aladdin and I was weary of the whole quest. The country turned to desert again and I rounded a dune and almost stepped on her. She scrambled up and let me have it.

'Watch where you're going! Who d'you think you are anyway? What are you doing round here?'

This tirade burst from her lips like wine from a broken bottle. She seemed oddly ageless as she yelled at me. On the one hand looking like a woman of some years, and yet at the same time having the vitality and vigour of someone much younger. It was as if her age had not yet stolen too much life from her.

'You should be careful!' she chided me, and she straightened her skirt and pulled at her sleeves.

She turned and marched away. Then she stopped suddenly and looked back.

'You're not another one of them are you?'

'Another one of what?'

She narrowed her dark eyes, put a hand to the hard line of her mouth. It was a shame I thought, about her anger, it spoilt her very obvious beauty.

'I didn't laugh you know,' she said. 'I didn't.'

'Fine. I believe you.'

She ran back to me and grabbed my wrists.

'Do you? Because I really need that. I need someone to believe me. Life is taking me into such strange places now.'

'Tell me about it.' I said, thinking more of myself than her. But the irony was lost on her.

'I will, I will tell you about it.' She sat and patted the sand next to her. Seems I had no choice. As I dropped down beside her I studied her sideways and took a closer look. She looked like the kind of woman who had grown into disappointment over the years.

'Are you hungry?' she said, 'because I should feed you. We always feed visitors. You know that don't you?'

She handed me some dried meat from a bag on her shoulder. She set the bag down and started up again.

'You don't know the pressure we're under. Walking off into the unknown chasing an invisible God. It feels so precarious. We have nothing. Nothing! No idols, no writings, no charts. He tells me he hears regularly from this God. But I don't know. I want to trust him all the time but I feel so stretched, so pulled apart by it, like I'm about to snap. Nothing is familiar anymore. The unknown never seems to become ordinary. I can't stop expecting it to become familiar, but it never does. Day after day there's something new. And then Egypt!' She threw up her hands. 'My hero husband gets wind of a food shortage and goes tearing off to break bread with the enemy. That was so frightening. Not for him – for me! He dumped me in Pharaoh's harem, you know? I don't think that notion came up in his conversations with the invisible God.

Oh no. that was his bright idea. He got all scared because we were running out of food, and instead of talking to his God he hatched a plan to run to Egypt. But then having got there he decided we should lie about our marriage in case his life was in jeopardy. So suddenly I'm just his sister.' She beat on the sand with her fist. 'Just his sister! After all we've been through...' and her words melted into sobbing, her face twisted with despair and for the first time her age showed a little. She leant on me and continued crying for a while. Then, when the sobbing subsided, she said, 'This is why I laughed. Because of all this. Because of the unknown and the deception and the invisible God and nothing being reliable anymore. That's why I laughed.'

I left a silence then said, 'But I thought you said you didn't laugh.'

'I didn't. Well...'

Now she left a silence. 'You don't understand,' she said after a while, her voice sadder, quieter. 'It's so hard, so hard to keep believing. It sounds so outrageous, so ludicrous, so... unbelievable. All my life I've longed for a family, and now there's talk of it, it seems preposterous. Every night he goes outside and looks up. He says it reminds him, keeps him going when he doubts. All those stars, one day he says his descendants will be as numerous.'

'I'm not one of them, you know,' I told her.

'One of the descendants?'

'One of the angels. That visited you.'

She looked at me as if I'd pelted her with water. 'You're not?'

'No. Far from it. I can't do anything. I can't make this any easier for you. I'm just a traveller like you.'

She gave a resounding, body-quaking sigh. It seemed to well up from her deepest, darkest place.

'You're not like us,' she said. 'You'll reach a destination and carry on with your life. Everything we once knew is on hold. Forever. There'll be no arriving, it'll always be about the journey now. I want some normality again.'

She rubbed the back of her left hand, I noticed a dry patch of eczema had formed there. She scratched it and then rubbed at her right elbow. Serious friction, as if she was trying to remove a difficult stain.

'And there's Hagar,' she went on, 'worst idea I ever had. I thought it would solve everything. Stop the wandering so we could settle down. Let her have the baby instead of me. But it's made no difference. Except that she lords it over me. I tell her off, she's no place to talk like she does and show off her boy to everyone. But she doesn't take any notice, she was a help to me in Egypt, she kept me going when it all seemed so dark. But now, now she *is* the darkness. I didn't laugh, well I did, but so would you. So would anyone.'

She seemed haunted by it. I ate some of the food she had given me, that seemed to cheer her a little.

'Will God curse me now?' she said. 'Because I laughed at him. I'll never have the baby now will I?'

'I don't think God's like that,' I said, sounding as if I knew something about it all. As if I was an expert in these things. But I went on, because she needed hope and because something in the atmosphere was urging me to encourage her. 'It says somewhere that he's patient and compassionate, slow to get mad with us, we have to hang onto that. It says so in the writings.'

'What writings?'

I wanted to say the Psalms, but that would achieve nothing. She and Abraham had nothing in writing. They had nothing but a voice calling them on.

'Where I come from we have a collection of sacred writings, we call it the Bible or the Good Book. Parts of it promise that this invisible God is one of love, a creator who understands and forgives.' It was the kind of thing I wanted someone to tell me. The kind of thing I wanted to be able to take hold of and grip with all my might, deep down in my being. She leant back and took a look at me.

'Are you a prophet of this invisible God?' she said.

'No! I've met a few lately and I'm not. No way.'

'But you talk about him in different terms.'

I laughed. 'I'm no hero.'

'You don't have to be a hero to be a prophet. My husband thinks he's a hero and he doesn't sound like you.'

'I come from somewhere else that's all,' I told her.

'A place where people speak about God an awful lot.'

'The invisible God? The one without any images or idols?'

'Sort of. Some people believe in that God but other people believe in lots of other gods.'

'Do they war about it?'

I considered and nodded. 'Sadly yes. Words, weapons. Whatever.'

'My father-in-law makes idols,' she said. 'It's easier to believe in things that you can see and touch, don't you think? Why would Abraham's God be invisible? And unnamed?'

Tough question. 'I don't know, but if everything else is made by him then I guess things that people turn into idols are actually supposed to merely point us to the great Creator. A bit like…' I fumbled for a metaphor, 'a… a divine cell phone hooking us up to God.'

'A what?'

Ah, awkward. More fumbling for a metaphor. 'Like a piece of written text, I guess. Or a picture. A work of art. Anything created points us to the one who created it. The artist. So with this created order. It points us to the one who created it.' I was on a roll now, surprising myself. *Preaching* to myself. 'The good things we see and encounter are like living letters, informing us and inviting us to know the one behind and beyond them.' I paused. She looked unconvinced so I added, 'Wouldn't you say?'

She shook her head and said, 'You've lost me.' Then she grimaced. 'I feel sick. I've felt it for the past week. Especially in the mornings. You're a prophet, am I ill?'

'I'm not a prophet but... at a guess I'd say... well... maybe you're... pregnant?'

And she laughed. Loud and heartily, and there was no way she could deny it. But it was healthy laughter, and by the time she had finished there were tears on her cheeks.

I stood up, something in me was telling me to move on.

'Thank you,' she said.

'For what? I couldn't do anything.'

She smiled. 'You did enough.'

I went.

17. Gideon

Another hole in the ground. More falling, more bruises and another landing on someone. This time I struck something sharp as I went. It grazed my side as I landed in a skewed mess on the floor.

'Watch it?' said a voice and I looked at a figure brandishing a shovel.

He waved it like a weapon. There was grain on his freckled features and stalks in his dark spiky hair. He looked about seventeen.

'What do you want?' he demanded. 'I'm doing nothing illegal here.'

I stood up and looked around. The place was barely big enough to do anything, illegal or not. I had disturbed a pile of grain on the floor. He spotted me looking at it and scooped it away with his shovel.

'I'm doing nothing,' he said.

'Why d'you look so guilty then?' I said.

He bit his lip then spat some chaff from his mouth.

'It's just food all right? People are hungry round here and there's nothing wrong with trying to feed them.'

'Fine,' I said, 'good idea.'

'Good.'

He stared at me, I considered telling him to carry on but he could hardly do that if I was down there with him, separating grain must have been hard enough in a hole in the ground, with me down there it was impossible. I reached for a handgrab and found a rock halfway up the wall. I pulled myself up and climbed out. He said nothing. As I walked away I heard him shovelling grain again.

'Not so quick,' said a voice.

It was the woman in white, the one I'd seen in the city sitting on the edge of the water trough. Same short black hair, a round face and rosy cheeks. Definitely her. I looked all around as if I expected to see a flash car or a bike. A Lambretta maybe. I could imagine someone like her riding a Lambretta, or a Vesper.

'I don't need a Lambretta,' she said, somehow reading my mind. 'I have my own form of transport.'

'You haven't brought that donkey again have you?' I said.

She laughed and her cheeks shone and turned a little more rosy.

'Nice thought,' she said. 'But no. However, it wouldn't do any harm for you to spend a little more time with Gideon.'

'Gideon?'

She wagged her thumb towards the hole in the ground. 'He needs a bit of encouragement. Feels like the world's against him. His family's a bit downtrodden and they're always on at him for being the smallest. What they don't know is he's about to change the world. You could help that.'

'Why should I?'

She recoiled a little, took a step back, put her hands on her hips and scowled.

'Odd,' she said, 'I hadn't taken you for mean-spirited. In fact you seemed to be mellowing with every turn of the page.'

'What page?'

'These pages, the ones you're trekking across. Look, there are bigger things going on, more than you know. It's always like that. We're asking you to join in that's all. Just like you did for Sarah back then.'

'Sarah? You mean the woman who didn't laugh?'

'Yep. You did a good job there. Made the invisible God visible for her. We like that.'

'We?' I looked around. 'Who's we?' I said.

'This lot.'

She raised a finger and swivelled it around as if there were some great crowd in the sky. I looked up and saw nothing.

'Believe me, this place is awful crowded if you could only see it. And they all like you.'

I didn't like that. Didn't want to be monitored like that.

She flapped a hand. 'You've nothing to worry about. It's up to you. Help, don't help. Talk to Gideon, don't talk to him. It's your call. But let's face it, you're not in a hurry to get anywhere are you?'

'Yes!' I yelped, taking a step towards her. 'I'm in a big hurry to find Aladdin and get out of here.'

'All in good time, all in good time. You wouldn't

want to spend so much time looking for the way out that you missed the adventure would you? Or maybe you would. A lot of people do.'

'Why not send the donkey? He seems to have plenty to say.'

'Down there? He'd be like a bull in a china shop.'

I looked back at the well.

'What do I have to say?' I said.

'You don't have to say anything. Just do what you do well – be interested. He's about to get a call from me, and that will give him a shock. Just nudge him along a little. Give him some lunch.'

She threw me a bundle of food. I sighed and sauntered back towards the well.

'I suppose I could,' I said.

There was no reply and when I looked back she'd gone. No Lambretta or Vesper, just the sound of a finger snapping and she was no more. I looked back down at Gideon. He was wiping his brow.

'Hungry?' I called.

He looked up startled, then frowned. 'You again.'

'I brought you some lunch,' I said.

'Really? Why?'

'It's not poisoned,' I assured him and dropped the packet down to him. He caught it awkwardly.

'Why?' he said again, sniffing at a handful of dates.

'Let's just say we're both in a fix. I'm sympathising.'

'You mean – the Midianites?'

I climbed back down the well. Gideon dropped his

shovel and slumped in a corner with the food. He seemed to quickly lose his fear and began shoving it down.

'You don't know about David and Goliath do you?' I said.

'David and who?'

'Goliath. Big giant of a guy. Ugly, and mean too.'

'You've met him?'

'Well no, I never actually saw him but you always assume the bad guys are ugly and mean don't you? Could be a complete sham of course, I'm sure there are plenty of cool and goodlooking monsters out there. Anyway, the point is, David was a small guy, about your age I think, who took on a giant and killed him. Everyone else was scared, including the king who was the tallest guy in the land and really should have stepped up to fight. You know, a one on one thing, the biggest guy on each side does battle to save a bloodbath and settle the outcome. Anyway, David was like you, a small guy battling a massive enemy.'

He looked worried, his freckled forehead creased up like a well-worn sheet.

'I'm not doing battle. I'm just making grain. I'm not looking for a fight. Look at me. I'm no giantkiller. If you want to fight Midianites go ahead but I won't be there.'

I laughed and his worry lines grew.

'What's funny?' he snapped.

'You. You're more capable than you know,' I said.

'Suppose I told you people will flock to follow you one day? What d'you think about that?'

'I think you're mad. Delusional.'

'Someone said I was a prophet recently.'

He shrugged. 'Don't know about that.'

'Suppose God asked you to do something difficult?' I asked.

'I am doing something difficult,' he said. 'Have you ever tried threshing grain in a hole in the ground with no wind around? When you thresh grain you throw it in the air and the breeze takes the chaff. There's no air down here. It's taking forever and it clogs up your lungs.'

He coughed right on cue.

'But you're still doing it and that's got you noticed,' I said.

He threw down the last of the food.

'I don't know what you're on about,' he said.

'Would you like to be a hero?' I said.

A sudden spark flashed in his eye, but he said, 'Nope.'

I didn't believe him. 'I don't think you know yourself very well. You watch, you'll be more than you think you are.'

I'd had enough and I reached for the handgrab again and hauled myself out. The woman in white was back. Sitting cross-legged near the mouth of the hole. She smiled at me.

'I did nothing,' I said.

'You did plenty,' she replied and she got up and started climbing in.

As I walked away I heard her say, 'Hi there, mighty man!' and I heard a heartfelt yelp from Gideon.

18. Isaiah

He rolled up in an old corroded sports car – a brown rust bucket of a classic. I'm no car man so I'd be guessing at the make and model. Let's just say it was an auto oxymoron. Clearly a star in its day, but now gone to seed. Drips of brown moisture dropped from the exhaust as it pulled up ahead of me.

'Give you a lift?' he called.

He had a tidy goatee, surfer blond hair and ear studs. I figured it was worth the chance. I'm normally too cautious to go hitching in life, but this wasn't life.

'I'm trying to write this poem,' he said as we pulled away and the wind snagged at his hair. The car picked up speed, but then coughed and lost it again. The whole journey turned out to be like this. Bursts of life ambushed by jolting, throaty groans.

'I'm no poet,' I said.

'Everyone's a poet, pal,' he said. 'They just don't know it.' He changed gear, the car growled and lurched, so he changed back again. 'So,' he went on, 'This poem of mine. It's about battling through the hard days of life. The empty years, the lonely nights, that sort of thing. You want to hear what I got so far? I need a sounding board.'

'Why not?'

'Do not be afraid…'

'I'm not.'

He laughed. 'No pal, this is the poem.'

He hit the accelerator and we speeded up, then the exhaust spat watery smoke and we slowed down again.

'Do not be afraid,' he said, 'for I've ransomed you.
I have called you by name; you're mine.
When you go through deep waters I will be with you.
When you battle through great trouble, I'll be there.
When you travel through rivers of difficulty, you will not drown.
When you walk through the fire of oppression, you will not be burned up.'

Silence, apart from the throaty roar of the engine. The wind blew dust on our faces then gusted it off again.

'What d'you think, pal?' he said eventually.

'It's good. What's it mean?'

'It's about the divine presence. You see I figure that people expect that when God is there, life is good. I want to tell them, that God is there, when life is hard. When it's bitter and twisted. When it threatens to crush and destroy. He's no less present when you're cornered and struggling.'

I considered this and nodded. 'And that will help people?'

'Some. For some it'll be a great comfort... for others... not so much. It might even annoy them. But maybe that annoyance will be like grit in an oyster, niggling away until the pearl takes shape.'

'Is that the whole of it?'

'Mmmm, for now. I get lots of stuff like this. Must keep a record of it all.'

He revved the engine again and the car leapt.

'In a hurry,' he said, 'got a slot booked at poet's corner.'

'With your poem?'

'Not that one, another one about a child. Want to hear that?'

I did.

'To us a child is born, to us a son is given. He will be called the prince of peace and he will rule with justice. He'll be full of wisdom and understanding. Never judging by hearsay or false truths. He will defend the poor and the oppressed. His day will be one of peace. The lion and the lamb will lie down together. And the earth will be filled with the presence of God.' He paused. 'Something like that. I never know until I get up there exactly how it'll come out.'

'Why not? D'you improvise?'

'Kind of, I listen. To the people and for the whisper of God.'

'Who's it about?' I asked.

'You know, I don't know. Sometimes a poet speaks of things he can't fathom. He just offers.'

'But what are you trying to make people do?'

'I'm not much making them do anything. I'm trying to be obedient.'

'To what?'

'The call. Of God. Believe me that's not easy. Last

year I went buff naked.'

I laughed. I'm not sure he appreciated it.

'Don't knock it pal, it got a response.'

'Yea. I'll bet.'

He slowed down.

'You have to get out here,' he said.

'Why?'

'No idea pal, I'm just getting a hunch. This is your stop. I'm Isaiah by the way.' He held out a grubby hand and we shook. I noticed he had oil in the grooves of his palm and snatches of poetry inked all over the back.

Then I got out. At my 'stop'. He waved and hit the accelerator, which caused the car to lurch forward, spit smoke, and die. He gave an embarrassed shrug, started it up again and drove off, a little more cautiously this time, the car spluttering and gasping as he went. And there I was by the road alone. Then I heard the sound of a wild animal and a fierce wind began to kick up. Somewhere in the distance there was the sound of pages fluttering and flicking over in the gusts. The sand rose up and spun around me. It whisked me off my feet, a little like Dorothy in *The Wizard of Oz*. I wasn't sure for a moment if I was headed for Kansas. Then I landed in a heap on hard ground. I pulled myself together and stood up. I was in a circular enclosure with epic stone walls. The place was gloomy and full of shadows, and there was no sign of Judy Garland.

19. Daniel

It was one of those moments when you can't figure if you're dreaming or not. And somehow pinching myself seemed too obvious, too much of a cliché. So instead I stood there staring at the beasts. They looked hungry but they weren't moving. One yawned, another belched. A kind of ravenous, feline belch, its jaws opening like a jagged mantrap to let the sour gas rush out. I was close enough to smell it. I'd have run but it felt as if someone had nailed my feet to the floor. Plus my insides were like water and I was terrified of spilling something. I heard a voice, somewhere between a whisper, a song and a sigh. A strange sound.

'O Lord, don't keep your distance. You're my strength here. Rescue me from a violent death; spare my precious life from these dogs. Snatch me from the lions' jaws.'

I turned, there was a man on his knees. His eyes closed, his fists tightly clenching each other. The knuckles were white and his face was white. There was not a lot of blood left in him. His lips were still moving, he seemed to be repeating himself. I guess he was praying and wondered if I should join him. I looked back to see one of the lions had stood and moved a step closer. Should you run from a lion or stay put? I couldn't remember which way round it was. Some animals attacked if you made a move, some just took a bite if you stood around long enough.

'O Lord, don't keep your distance. You're my strength here. Rescue me from a violent death…'

'Me too Lord,' I called, and the sound of my voice made all the lions sit up and take notice. I realised why the other guy had been praying so softly.

He opened his eyes. They were old and reddened. He was clearly under stress, had been a for a while. He looked old for his time, his beard and hair white, his skin wrinkled and tight against his skull. He took one look at me, leapt up and backed away, pressing tight against the den wall. Apparently I scared him more than the lions.

'Who are you?' he asked in his soft squeaky voice. 'What are you doing here? Are you…' he bent towards me and crept closer, 'from God?'

'No, but I am.'

It was her. The woman in white. She was standing right beside the largest lion, the one who had belched and was now moving closer. She looked as if she was just out for a stroll with a poodle. She ran a hand through the creature's mane and stroked its back.

'One day lions and people will be at peace again,' she said, 'as in the early days.'

'Are we in danger?' I said.

She laughed and it made the lion roar. I backed away and pressed against the wall beside the other guy.

'Of course you're in danger. These creatures will eat you before you can say *Lion Bar*. That's why they've thrown Daniel in here. That's the plan.'

We both slid down the wall at that point, our legs giving way. I could smell the fear on both of us. It was not pleasant.

'What are we going to do?' I whispered to the old guy.

He swallowed hard. 'I only have one option,' he said. 'I have to pray.'

He moved his lips quietly, framing a language I didn't recognise. I took a look around. The den was circular and stone and the doors looked very shut. Plus they were across the enclosure from us and there were a lot of lions in the way. The woman in white stood there, still stroking the lion's head.

'How did you get in here?' I asked.

'Through the doors, but they're locked now.'

'No. I meant – why are you in here?'

'Praying.'

'I know you are, but why are you in here?'

'For praying.'

'For praying?'

'Of course.'

He offered a weak smile as he looked at me and rubbed a shaking hand across his mouth.

'I pray towards Jerusalem every day. Three times. It's my lifeline. I feel a long way from home sometimes.'

I looked at the lions. Right then, I knew how he felt.

'The king passed a law decreeing that no one could worship anyone except him for a month. I can't comply with that. I can't. I respect the king, I honour him. But I respect God and honour him more.'

'But if it's just for a month…'

He held up his wrinkled hand and I noticed it wasn't shaking now.

'I won't compromise. I can't. I'm scared and I don't want to be attacked by these lions. But something inside me tells me what is right.'

'You'd die for praying?' I said.

He nodded and as he did the big lion roared at us.

'Would you die for anything?' he said.

The bridge. His question was like a transporter, sending me right back in time and space. I lied.

'I don't know,' I mumbled.

The lion roared again and suddenly lurched at us but then yelped as she grabbed its mane and pulled it in line. She grabbed its jaws and squeezed them together. A second roar came out as a squeak.

'No one's dying today,' she said. 'I'll see to that. Your prayers have been answered old man. Those and the prayers of another. You have an odd ally.'

He looked at me but I shrugged. The woman in white laughed. 'No,' she said, 'not him. Stranger than that.'

'Who then?'

She smiled and her face turned a bright shade of rosy. 'The king. He never wanted you dead Daniel. He was tricked by his "loyal right-hand men".'

She lifted her hands and framed the phrase with quotation marks from her fingers, but as she did so the lion took his chance and leapt at us. His mouth loomed large and deadly, like a cave of razors. The woman in white lunged and brought him down with a rugby tackle just inches from my face. She dragged him back to the others by the tail and snapped her fingers. He turned instantly dozy and lay down. Seconds later he and the others were asleep.

'Sorry about that,' she said, pulling out a brush and brushing her hair back into place. 'Should have done that earlier. I was trying to be too clever. Showing off as usual. Were you impressed with my rugby tackle?'

We were both in shock and it was hard to communicate anything with our bodies rigid and our mouths wide. She laughed again and strolled over to us. She closed the old guy's mouth and rearranged my shoulders, then she squatted down in front of us.

'You'll be fine,' she said, 'now where was I? Oh yes, the king. He hasn't eaten a thing all night. He's been fasting for you guys. Well not for you,' she said nodding towards me, 'he doesn't know you. But for Daniel. He's been awake and fasting. Doesn't want to lose you. I guarantee that you'll both walk out of here free and alive. And when you do Daniel, that king of yours will surprise you with his acknowledgement of your God.' She thought for a moment. 'Except it won't be a surprise now as I've just forewarned you. Sorry about that.' She turned and pointed across the enclosure. 'Those gates will be opened soon, and you'll be able to leave. The lions won't bother you, they'll sleep it off now. I suggest you guys get some sleep. You both look rough.' She smiled and patted my shoulder. 'See you again,' she said and she walked past the lions and out through the locked gates.

Daniel let out a long, protracted sigh and slowly relaxed. I was about to speak when I noticed his eyelids dropping. He adjusted his position and rested his head against the wall. A few minutes later he was out. I tried to follow his lead but couldn't crack it. I kept opening one eye to check those lions were still horizontal, somehow I couldn't quite relax with four sleeping man-eaters in the room. I got up, strolled to the far gates and checked the lock. They weren't going to open. Not without a rocket launcher. I stepped back to get a better view of the high wall and that's when I did it. Crushed the tail of the biggest lion. He let out a roar and leapt to his feet. It took him a split second to spot the perpetrator and he came right at me. I've often wondered how spiders manage to clamber up a vertical wall, well, somehow they do, as somehow I did. I hurled myself upwards, grabbed at a few stony lumps and got myself as high up as possible. But it wasn't enough, I could feel my scrabbling feet slipping and that lion was adamant it was lunchtime. That's when the rope hit me on the nose. I grabbed it and someone pulled on the other end with the greatest of ease. In a second I was sitting astride the enclosure wall watching the woman in white tutting. She looked down at the pacing lion, placed her finger and thumb in the air and snapped them together. The beast crumpled and cracked his chin on the ground as he fell back into sleep.

'What were you doing?' she hissed at me. 'Have you no patience?'

'I couldn't sleep. Too scared of Leo down there.'

'His name's Parsley and he's a big softie really. Come on.'

She grabbed my shoulder and somehow we landed on the safe side of the wall. She pointed away from civilisation.

'That-a-way,' she said.

'Thanks for saving me,' I said.

She rolled her eyes. 'Like I said,' she pointed her finger at the skies and rolled it around, 'you're not alone in this. You have a great crowd of witnesses cheering you on. It's like Glastonbury up there.'

I looked up and saw nothing. It was unnerving. When I looked down she had gone.

20. Ezekiel Again

I was dirty and battered, tired and sweating now. My hands and knees were scuffed and scored from scrambling up the den wall, plus my side was throbbing from my fall into Gideon's well. I had walked for a few hours and had no idea where I was going. I couldn't get the image of being watched out of my head. The woman in white had spooked me a little. I thought I'd just opted to come on a weird adventure with Aladdin, she made it sound like much more. I didn't like that. I felt out of control. I just wanted to get back to the safety of the world I knew. I thought about Sarah and her fears about the unknown. I'd sounded so confident talking to her. How did I do that? Talk so big and walk so small? I was berating myself about this when I heard the distant rumbling, a clattering sound of stones and broken trees gathering momentum and washing my way.

Rattle slosh clack thud. The ground shook and the air turned damp but I could see nothing. I looked around for a place to shelter. I could do with Gideon's hole now. Nothing. I looked to the sky and called out a muddled prayer. Maybe the talking donkey would ride by and I could hitch a lift. The rumbling noise grew and as I stared the horizon turned watery. I was going to drown. Maybe that would be my way back home. Get washed away in this world and end up back in the other one. That would do for me. The end of everything here and a whole new start over there. I stood my ground and waited. The water became more visible as it kept coming, pouring towards me. Bits of things protruded from the surface, a vast sea of detritus being washed along with the oncoming tide. And suddenly there, up to his neck and puffing like mad, was that prophet again. The one in the bright blue trousers, the flower shirt and headband. He was back again from his valley of death. He disappeared below the surface, then his blue legs appeared, quickly followed by the rest of him, splashing and squirming about. He spotted me and called out, waving as he did so.

'Another vision,' he cried, as if it was the most natural thing, 'a watery one.'

That was an understatement. Another wave hit him and he disappeared again. I stood my ground and before long the waves crashed over me, knocking me backwards and under the surface. I felt my bones colliding with branches and small rocks. Then my legs wrapped themselves around an arm and a hand grabbed my foot. We disentangled and both surfaced at the same time, coughing and spluttering.

'It's okay,' he said, 'it's the water of life. We won't drown.'

I wasn't so sure.

'Don't fight it,' he called, 'go with it. Let it carry you along. If you struggle you'll sink.'

He scooped up a passing gnarled branch and threw it at me, it bounced off my head and I clung on to it. He grabbed one himself and we surfed along awkwardly. The torrent went on for a while, eventually washing us up on a dirty, littered beach. We crawled ashore and sat with our backs against a a couple of slimy rocks. My head was pounding from the impact of the branch. We said nothing, just waiting there, catching our breath. As the water lapped over the sand the beach began to change colour. The grey turned a lively yellow, and bits of dead branches somehow took root and began to grow again. The weather warmed up and the sun set about drying us off with the help of a suitably keen breeze. Green shoots appeared and before long the scrawny beach had become a lush wonderland, vibrant with greens, blues and reds. Incredibly rare and beautiful birds appeared and took rest in the newly sprouting branches. There was the buzz of insects and the cry of small animals. The place blossomed and flourished in a matter of minutes.

'What is this?' I said. 'What's going on?'

He pulled off his headband and wrung the water from it. He looked to the sky and listened for a moment.

'Like I said,' he muttered, 'living water. Wherever it goes, things come back to life.'

'Where's it come from?'

'The temple. God's home. Like I said, it's another

vision.'

He tugged his headband back on. A few dribbles of water slipped from it and ran down the bridge of his nose.

I felt my side itching and pulled up my shirt. The scrape from Gideon's shovel had stopped throbbing, plus it was fading as I watched. At the same time the wounds on my hands and knees from the lion's den were easing and subsiding.

'Can I see this temple?' I said.

'You can see it but you can't go in, at least not very far in.'

'Why not?'

'Only the high priest can come close to God. It's the way.'

'But isn't God everywhere?'

The prophet pursed his lips and considered this.

'King David had a vision and his son made it real. A home for God. A magnificent temple.'

'But things change.'

'What things?'

'Well look around, God's here, isn't he? He flooded this place and resurrected it.'

The prophet nodded. 'It's true, this does go beyond expectations.'

'So you deliver messages, without understanding them?'

'Of course. It's not my job to understand. It's my job to communicate. That's what a prophet is, the voice of God to the people. If I could understand everything I'd be God. And I'm not.'

I couldn't help thinking of Isaiah with his spluttering rust bucket, and the poem he recited but didn't understand. The one about the prince of peace.

'How d'you get this job in the first place?' I asked Ezekiel.

He snorted. 'Having the right personality, being stubborn and obnoxious and not afraid of looking an idiot. Having no friends helps, 'cause then you're not afraid of losing them. Plus I saw a vision that was terrifying and inspiring. All smoke and cloud it was, and these cherubim with wheels and wings and faces.'

'What sort of faces?'

He shut his eyes and I guess he travelled back in time.

'A lion, an ox, an eagle, and a man.'

He sat very still and drank in the memory of his vision. I thought of the tattoo I'd seen on the warrior in the gleaming armour. Four faces etched on his arm. The same four faces.

He sighed. 'Terrible and incredible,' he said after a while, 'graceful and grandiose.' And he opened his eyes and made himself smile.

'But suppose you're wrong?' I asked. 'With your messages? Suppose your own agenda gets in the way?'

'Then I pay the price. A false prophet is punished by the people.'

I thought about Jeremiah in his well. 'Maybe a true prophet can be punished too. The people can get it very wrong.'

'Absolutely, it's a precarious job, don't volunteer. That's my advice. Most of the time, if you tell the truth, people don't want you. They are often like sheep without a shepherd, herding one way then another. It's always been the way. They'd rather follow each other than a prophet, it's more attractive to run after the latest big thing.'

I thought about recent popular fads. The rise of those bushy, hipster beards and *Fifty Shades of Grey*.

'Not much changes,' I said. 'Peer pressure seems to turn everything into a quest for entertainment where I come from.'

'I try to tell them,' he said, 'I gathered a crowd one night and told them they only come and hear me for an evening out. A bit of cheap entertainment. What will the local prophet say tonight that's shocking and outrageous? They listen and smile and nod and then they go home, eat, drink, laugh and forget. It's as if they look in a mirror, see mud on their cheeks and then walk away and do nothing. And of course, what did the crowd do when I told them that? Listened to me, smiled and nodded, then went home to eat, drink, laugh and forget. Crazy'

I thought about the many times I'd looked in the

mirror and seen mud and just walked away. 'We eat, drink and laugh in order to forget the mud,' I said quietly.

'Well, we'd better wake up. Otherwise why have prophets? If people keep ignoring them maybe all the prophets will just melt away.'

The water began to recede and as it did so the sand lost its lively yellow glow. The colours faded as the trees began to wither and the extraordinary wildlife took flight. My heart sank as so much grey crept back. Glum-featured clouds muted the sunny warmth, but we were dried out by now. The prophet sighed and shook his head.

'That's that,' he said. 'Time to talk to the people. Tell them about the vision. You coming?'

He stood and offered me his hand. I shook my head. I had that moving on feeling again.

'Time to get going,' I said, 'I have my own vision to pursue.' Whatever that was.

I watched him wander off then stayed in that grim grey place for a while, jotting down random notes in my moleskine notebook. Eventually I tucked it away and walked on.

21. Esther

I came across a city. Another one. It just sort of rose up out of the road I was on. All columns and domes and carvings. The architecture was ornate and spectacular, quite different to anything I'd encountered so far. I slipped in through the arch of a side gate and headed for the sound of a crowd. The noise grew and I came to a large square filled with people. Some kind of spectacle, maybe some street entertainment. If so, these performers were good, the place was jammed. I edged my way through the bodies, intent on getting a better view. I wished I hadn't. There was a gallows on a stage. Right there for everyone to see. Children, teenagers, old and young, frail and strong. A public execution. I didn't need that.

'What's going on?' I whispered to a woman nearby.

She looked at me, amazed. 'You don't know? Where have you been?'

I'd love to have told her but I doubt she was ready for that.

'The Prime Minister's coming,' she went on.

'Oh. Is he going to give a speech?'

She laughed. 'Doubt it, he won't have time.'

'Then what's...' I stopped as she looked at me and raised a painted eyebrow. The penny dropped. 'You don't mean... you do mean! What happened? Did he lose an election?'

She shook her head, but I got the feeling she had no

idea what I was talking about.

'His plot was exposed. The queen told the king.' She giggled and said, 'He built that gallows for his enemy Mordecai and now look. He'll be swinging on it instead!'

There was a roar as she said this and cheers as the prisoner was brought out. Still wearing the clothes of his office, he was led onto the platform looking very sorry for himself. I thought of Eglon. This killing may not have been as bloody but I wasn't sure I wanted to witness another leader biting the dust. I turned away.

'You look as if you could do with a good bathe,' she said.

Oh great. Another woman telling me to wash.

'I run the local baths, I'll do you a deal. Half price.' She held out her hand.

I dug into my pockets, mostly out of curiosity to see if I had anything in there. Sure enough I pulled out a handful of coins. Apparently the right ones as she fished through them with her painted fingers and pulled out three.

'Turn right over there and then left. It's obvious then. Miriam is on the door. Give her this and she'll show you the way.' She pushed a smooth pebble into my hand. It had a number on it. As I turned to go I heard the crowd explode again. I glanced back to see the Prime Minister's head slipping into the noose. I decided to get out of there before the final act. Too late, before I could look away there was a creak and a rasp and a roar from the crowd. I turned to leave as the body fell and the rope took the weight.

Miriam was dark and fierce. She was not to be trifled with. I handed her the pebble, she took one look and barked orders at me. Take that passage there and the next one on the left and then the third turning on the right. That sort of thing. As ever I switched off halfway through and figured I'd just take my chances. How hard can it be to find a bathroom? Pretty hard as it turned out. I had not been going long when I found myself hopelessly lost, standing at a four-way junction with no idea which way to turn next. I retraced my steps, thankfully managing to do that without too much meandering. As I drew near the entrance there was a shout and a scream and I rounded a corner to see an armoured guard lunging at Miriam with a knife. Thankfully my survival instincts, usually very strong indeed, trouble and I do their best to take different roads, did not kick in this time. I dropped my towel and threw myself across the tiled floor. My shoulder hammered into the guard's bulky midriff, winding him and knocking backwards. The knife clattered on the floor and Miriam screamed a second time. I also hit the floor. The guard leapt up, threw a punch at me that missed and took off. Miriam grabbed me and hugged me, her fierce exterior now just a memory.

'Thank you, thank you!' she gasped. 'He was going to kill me.'

'Why?'

She calmed down and disentangled herself from me.

'Haman's plot to kill us Jews. In spite of the Prime Minister's death I think this guy still wanted to carry it through.'

I stepped outside and checked the street. There was no sign of her attacker.

'Well he's gone now,' I said.

She wiped her face. 'Thank you,' she said again, 'you saved my life.'

'Should we report him?'

She thought for a moment then nodded.

'We should tell Esther. She's the queen. Just in case he tries again. Esther will know what to do, she foiled the plot in the first place.'

'But can you get an audience with the queen?'
She laughed. 'Of course! We grew up together. She'd better not refuse me or I'll tell the king a few bits of juicy gossip about her! Come on.'

She locked up the baths and headed back towards the square. She could move at a pace and I had to hurry to keep up. I threw a cursory glance towards the gallows as we passed. The body was there, swinging in the breeze.

True to her word Miriam took just ten minutes to get us into Esther's palace wing. We were marched by a couple of po-faced sentry-types into a roomful of silks and silvers. The ceiling was a single mosaic, a melodramatic montage of lovers and fighters. The sentries left us, Esther arrived and we bowed low. There was a respectful silence then Miriam hurled herself at the queen. The two hugged, laughed and exchanged a few in-jokes. Then Esther glanced at me and raised her exquisitely manicured eyebrows.

'A new hero on your arm?' she said.

Miriam giggled and introduced me.

'He saved my life,' she said, 'threw himself at the killer. He could have died. Honestly, he was a hero.'

Esther was extraordinarily beautiful, with her perfect complexion, strong cheek bones and a captivating, day-brightening smile. She took my hand and pressed it between hers.

'Thank you,' she said, 'you saved my best friend. Miriam,' she glanced at her friend. 'I'll send a guard to look after you for the next few days. Make sure he doesn't return. We may have to watch out for more of these. I think perhaps the king will need to issue something about the Jews defending themselves from such attacks. D'you think you could manage to do a sketch of his face perhaps? You were always a star with a piece of charcoal. I seem to recall you making very unflattering doodles of me!' Miriam shrugged and did her best to look innocent. She failed. Esther looked back at me. 'You must stay at the palace. I'll have the servants prepare a guest room, you can clean up and stay here as long as you would like. My guest of honour.'

I took a long look around at the overwhelming opulence and extravagant luxury, my head swam a little. I nodded. I might well stay a long time.

I had the best night's sleep. Twelve hours uninterrupted. No nightmares. I woke between satin sheets, ate breakfast in bed, took a long soak in a bath the size of a swimming pool and spent the rest of the morning idling in the sun. In the afternoon I took a stroll in Esther's private garden. She looked tired and we talked about the plot she had foiled. It had taken its toll on her.

'I never wanted to be here now. Some women would kill for this kind of life, but it was never about being queen. My cousin pushed me into it, he was convinced God was behind it all,' she smiled, 'I think he was right.' Then she sneezed. 'Oh, I think I'm getting a cold.' She pressed her palm to her forehead, checked her temperature. 'I wasn't made for this. Whatever my cousin might say. People see more in you than you see yourself I suppose. They look at you and see capability and confidence when really you're battling with reluctance and fear.'

That put me in mind of Frodo.

'I guess you don't know *Lord of the Rings*?' Of course she didn't. 'There's a quote I can only half remember about one character, Frodo, wishing he'd never landed where he had. He told his friend Gandalf.'

'And what did his friend Gandalf say?' she asked.

'I think he replied that many people wish the same thing,' I said, 'but all that was needed was for Frodo to decide what he would do with the time that had been given to him.' I thought about myself then. 'I reckon I might have used the time to punch Gandalf,' I said. 'Did you ever want to thump your cousin?'

She laughed and her beautiful face lit up. I turned and looked at her for too long. Seeing that smile break across her face was like watching a sunset on a spring morning. I could have looked all day.

'I could stay here forever,' I said, tearing my gaze away.

And then I woke up. Not between satin sheets and with breakfast in bed, but lying at an odd angle in some reeds near a river. The sun was beating down and yet again I had been transported whilst I slept. There had been no long soak in that right royal bathtub, no lazy morning in the palace. It was only dawn now and I was Gandalf-knows-where with my stomach rumbling and a film of early morning sweat already building up on my skin. I had been sleeping in my clothes and they were dirtier than ever. Great. I shut my eyes and took one last look at Esther. Then I heard other voices.

22. Shiphrah, Puah and Moses

And the crying of babies. I crept forward and peered through the reeds. Two women were standing by the river, each holding baskets. The crying was coming from inside. They swung the baskets back and prepared to throw them.

'After you Puah,' said the shorter of the two.

'I'm just getting ready,' the other said.

They put the baskets down and stretched, then picked them up and swung them back again. The babies continued crying. The one called Puah put her basket down.

'Why do I have to go first?' she demanded and as she spoke she leant over the basket and took out a tiny child. She held it to herself.

'What are you doing?' said the shorter woman.

'Just quietening him down. It's easier if he's not wailing.'

'No it's not, you're making friends with the child. Don't do that. You're making it harder for yourself.'

Puah put the child back into the basket. She crouched and picked it up again.

'We shouldn't waste the baskets Shiphrah,' she said. 'They're expensive. And besides, the baby might float down the river and be found by someone else. We want them to drown don't we?'

A pause then, 'Yes.'

Silence.

'Well, no,' Shiphrah said, 'I don't want them to drown. Pharaoh wants them to drown. We have dedicated our lives to helping children live. It's not our job to... to do this. Let Pharaoh kill babies if that's what he wants.'

'You know you'd never dare go to his palace and tell him that,' Puah snapped back. 'I mean – who would? Who'd dare stand before the king of kings and defy him to his face. If he says we have to kill children then we must do it or...'

'Or what?'

'You know. Face the consequences. Die ourselves. Pharaoh would think nothing of throwing two midwives in the river.'

'He wouldn't!' cried Shiphrah. 'We're too good at our job!'

'Not at the moment we're not! We've been ordered to kill baby boys and we're standing here yakking. And anyway, don't kid yourself. Pharaoh doesn't care about our skills. If we defy him we die. It's the way. Now come on.'

Puah picked up the basket again and prepared to hurl it into the water. Then she stopped.

'I've got an alternative idea,' she said. 'One that means none of us may die.'

'Go on.'

'Suppose we tell Pharaoh that whenever we arrive the Hebrew women have already hidden their babies. Tell him they give birth too quick for us. He hasn't got a clue about childbirth, he'll believe us.'

'I like that. To be honest, I couldn't live with myself if I did this. It's against God's law, I know it is, and I want to honour him, not Pharaoh. I'd be forever haunted.'

Puah laughed. 'D'you know what? I'm the same. I want to honour God. It's been in my mind all along. We're fools aren't we? Not saying anything about this to each other.'

'We have to take the risk. Save the babies and lie to Pharoah.'

'Wait a minute, I don't think God likes us lying either, does he?'

'Well,' Shiphrah looked off into the distance for moment, 'sometimes there are lies that preserve life. Non-selfish lies. That's what I say anyway. And did you never tell your husband he looked wonderful when he resembled a rubbish tip?'

They both laughed now. They took the crying babies from the baskets and cuddled them. The crying went on but the women looked happier. They looked about for any witnesses, I kept my head down, and they went. I started to stand up but it felt as if there was a hand on my shoulder holding me down. The next minute the clouds began to speed up, racing like dogs after a rabbit. The day suddenly ended and the night closed in as fast as someone flicking a switch. It lasted a few seconds then became another day with more racing clouds. Vague, indistinguishable figures flitted by the water then another night and another day and another night and another day. Time had lost all sense of proportion. In all of these nights passing I got no sleep. There was barely time to breathe. As the days flew by I swear I heard the sound of paper rustling and pages turning. Eventually the whole thing stopped abruptly and it was another dawn, and there they were again, the two midwives swapping notes. I felt as if I had jetlag.

'It's got worse hasn't it?' said Shiphrah

'Much.'

'You realise we've no chance of saving them now with this new law.'

'You've heard then? The world and his wife now ordered to snatch new-born boys. Can you believe it? Is Pharaoh so frightened of Hebrews?'

'Look out someone's coming.'

They ducked and slipped into the bushes. Right beside me. They immediately saw me there and stared with wide eyes. Puah opened her mouth to speak, but I pushed a finger against my lips. She shut her mouth. We watched, the midwives clocking me as much as the figures by the river.

Two women, one with a reed basket coated in tar. Done hastily by the looks of it. They looked around them as they came, as if they were doing something highly illegal. A baby gave a small cry and the other woman, a teenager actually – younger than I'd first thought – quickly leant in and distracted the child.

They knelt by the river, while the woman, the mother maybe, spoke quietly to the child and then looked to the heavens as if saying a silent prayer. Then they placed a cover on the basket and slid it into the water, hidden amongst a crowd of reeds. The two figures stepped away and hugged, then the mother whispered something to the teenager and she went, wiping her eyes as she hurried away. Before long other voices sounded and the baby cried. The teenager panicked, looked for a place to hide and hurled herself into the bushes. On the other side of me. She stared wide-eyed. I repeated my finger to the lips signal. It was getting crowded in there. Some kind of royal entourage appeared. A group of servant girls surrounding a woman of some standing. Her clothes, her make-up and hair were immaculate, I guessed this was Pharaoh's wife. Or his daughter perhaps. I hoped they didn't suddenly dive into the bushes, there'd be no room. We'd all be crushed. The baby cried again. The teenager beside me gave a whimper then clamped a hand across her own mouth. She looked terrified. Puah reached across me to try and comfort the girl. I got caught in the crossfire. Awkward. I ducked my head and wriggled out from between them. Puah closed the gap and Shiphrah looked at me as if it was all my fault.

'It's a child, your highness,' one of the servants was saying.

She had pulled the basket from the water and

removed the lid. The princess looked in and made all the right noises. She reached inside and scooped up the child.

'He is so sweet,' she said, 'poor thing, left here all alone like this. I'm going to adopt him.'

'He looks like one of the Hebrew babies, madam,' another servant said doubtfully.

'I don't care,' cooed the princess, 'I love him already. Look at his eyes, and he's stopped crying. It's clear, we have a connection.'

Puah leant close to the teenager.

'Miriam, go now. This is your chance. Offer to help. Go.'

The girl perked up, hesitated for a moment, then ran out of the bushes.

'Your highness,' Miriam bowed low, but couldn't contain her enthusiasm and shot straight back up without waiting for a response, 'I could find a Hebrew wet nurse to help you look after him. If it pleases your highness.'

The princess barely gave her a glance. She was all over the baby. 'It does, it does. Hurry along. One of my girls will go with you. But don't hurry back too quickly, I need some time with this little man.'

The princess sat down by the river cradling the baby in her arms. She started singing to him. Some song about him being chosen and unique.

Before long Miriam was back. With her own mother.

'I found a wet nurse, your highness,' she gasped

and she gave her mother a shove forward.

The servant girls looked at her and gave no sign of being impressed. But the princess tore her gaze away from the child's face and spoke to her.

'This is special boy, I can feel it. Look after him very carefully. Treat him well. I'll send you money and everything you need. When he's older I'll take him to the palace. You're under royal orders now, okay?'

The mother nodded as soberly as she could manage, but I guess there was a smile lurking somewhere behind her sombre expression. She took the baby and the basket and carried them away.

'Goodbye my little Moses,' the Princess called after them, 'I'll see you very soon, beautiful boy.'

It was an extraordinary turn around, I glanced at the midwives, they both had tears in their eyes. I stared at them.

'Well,' said Puah, 'why not? It's a touching outcome.'

Shiphrah sniffed. 'God's in this,' she said. 'I feel it.'

The princess turned back to the river and began removing her clothes for bathing.

Puah turned to me and cocked an eyebrow.

'I think that's your cue to leave, young man,' she said.

I didn't need telling twice, I wriggled back through the bushes and escaped.

23. Abigail

'Are you one of them?'

She was beautiful. But dressed down. As if she was doing her best to blend in. No sign of any make-up, and her clothes were drab and dowdy.

'Sorry?' I said.

'Sorry for what?' she said.

'No. I mean – I'm sorry I don't understand you.'

'Are you with the renegades? With David?'

I shook my head. 'I haven't seen anyone round here for a while. I'm trying to find my friend.'

She frowned and pressed a hand to her forehead, she had ash smeared across the back. I noticed then that she had ash on both hands.

'He's gone, you see,' she said. 'Dead.'

'David?'

'No. My husband. Nabal. I need to find David and his men. I need to tell them. Will you help me?'

I had nothing else to do right then. She pointed ahead and I turned and followed her.

'We'll get some provisions first, in case it takes a while. You look as if you could do with a good meal. Would you like a bath too?'

I shrugged. I didn't care. Not really. She put me in mind of Rahab, and that wasn't helpful.

'He was a fool, I know I shouldn't speak ill of him. But he brought this on himself. Wouldn't help others and spent his time eating and drinking and pleasuring. No wonder God took him.' She sighed and shook her head. 'A rich fool.'

And then she squatted down and started sobbing. I knelt beside her. Placed an arm gently around her. I could feel her body shudder with each sob. We stayed like that for a while.

'I'm sorry,' she said eventually, sniffing and wiping her face. 'He was an idiot but he was still my husband. And he wasn't always like that. Not when we were first married. He was a wiser man then.'

She stood up and sniffed again. She had ash smears across her cheeks now, from wiping them with the back of her hand.

'Success can change people, can't it? Dull their brains, twist their consciences. It did him anyway. He was fine when we were starting out, battling life together, being happy in our struggles and dreams. But once the dream became reality, once he had so much more to lose, then he altered. Started fretting about how he must hang on to his wealth. And that melted his brain, turned him stupid. You know he nearly got himself killed? David and his men needed help, but he refused. They could have murdered him. They wanted to, thank God I found out about it in time.'

'You saved him? How? What did you do?'

'Took them food and gifts to soften them up. And I persuaded them not to go ahead. David killing Nabal would have been a bad move for all of us. David included. I'm sure of it.'

She started walking again and said nothing for a while. She moved quickly, efficiently, and I had to hurry to keep up. I wanted to tell her about the ash smears on her cheeks but somehow couldn't find the confidence to speak up. Then a brief smile flashed across her lips.

'He has a kind face, that David. They say he's going to be king one day you know. I like him.'

'Is that why you want to find him?' I ventured.

She thought about this for a while. A house appeared on the horizon. It was big and sprawling. I could make out servants and farmhands moving around in the grounds.

'I have all this at the moment,' she said, 'but a woman alone round here is not a good thing. Men do what they want. Take what they want. That's why it's wise to find a good one and hang onto him.' She looked at me and nodded. 'Yes,' she said, 'I am planning what you're thinking. I will mourn and then I will marry. People say I'm beautiful. Perhaps that will be enough to win me a future king.'

She gave me the best meal I'd had in a long time. I never got the bath though. I had one foot in the water when the shout went up. Servants ran as horses' hooves came pounding. I grabbed my clothes and ran myself. They were outside, clustered in the shade at the front of the house. I hovered in a nearby doorway and watched as she bowed before him. He didn't look like a king. But he had the marks of a hero. His men were a bunch of scarred cut-throats. Not at all pretty like him. She bowed again and I noticed her cheeks were clean. I couldn't help wondering if she'd been annoyed that I hadn't mentioned the smears. I could hear them talking out there but couldn't catch what they were saying. I felt a movement beside me and turned to see a servant girl standing close.

'She'll do it,' she whispered, 'she'll get him. She's no fool, and she's wiser than him. He'd be an idiot to refuse her.'

And as she said this the future king stepped forward and took her hand. She led him towards the house and I figured it was time to leave. David and his men might be quite happy round her, but I wasn't so sure they'd be quite so taken with me. I found a window and climbed through it.

24. Samson

A handsome thug. It's the best way I can think of to describe him. The thought hit me like a train as soon as I saw him. He was clearly a renegade, and one far too goodlooking for his good. With his flowing hair, impressive torso and his perfectly placed features. He mugged me as I was walking down a quiet road. On my way to another town he leapt out and demanded some spare cash. He wasn't overly aggressive and had no weapons, but then he didn't need any, his very presence was powerful enough. I was happy to give him what I had, parting with money here was never a problem as (a) I never knew what I'd find in my pockets and (b) I didn't feel like I had any claim to these strange currencies anyway.

'Let's go out,' he said, 'find a good inn and burn the midnight oil.'

He laughed uproariously as if he'd made a side-splitting joke.

'I don't want to go drinking,' I mumbled.

'Neither do I,' he roared, and he looked suddenly serious as death.

'Never drunk a drop in my life,' he said. 'I'm a man of restraint.' And then he laughed again. 'Sort of.'

He dragged me to a bar he knew in a nearby town and we stayed up all night feasting, eating eating eating; man that guy had an appetite. I kept up with him by nibbling at the edges, while Samson sat there bragging about his conquests. They were many and colourful in detail to say the least. He may not have drunk wine but he had a raging thirst for women.

'Let's steal the city gates,' he said, his eyes ablaze with alcohol and arrogance. 'I did it once before, after spending a night with a whore. The locals couldn't believe their eyes. Let's do it again.'

He slammed his hands on the table, spilling both drinks and pushed himself upwards out of his seat. He staggered for a moment then steadied himself and hoiked a thumb towards the door.

'Come on,' he barked.

He kicked open the door with single swipe of his foot. The door burst wide, struck the wall and slammed back in place, smacking Samson on the forehead as it did so. He wasn't deterred, he kicked it again and was ready for the rebound this time, with his hand up to stop the rebounding door. The dawn was beginning to break out there.

'We can't do this, people will see,' I said, my words slurring into one another.

'Who cares? No one will catch us. God is on our side.'

I followed him up the hill to the gates, like a downtrodden donkey dragged after its master. Not long back I was being hailed as a prophet, now look at me, a weak-minded, insecure idiot, about to cause criminal damage. Samson reached the gates way before I wanted him to, he stretched his arms the length of one of the gates and tore it from the post with a single tug. It looked as if he was pulling up a few blades of grass.

'Grab the other one,' he ordered.

I took hold but there was no way I was repeating his little miracle. The gate didn't budge. He threw back his head and roared with laughter. 'You spindly muscled weakster,' he said. 'Hold this.'

He dropped his gate right beside me and I did my best to keep it upright, then he grabbed the other gate and tore it from its moorings with a single swipe. There was a shout from below and we looked at the bottom of the hill to see three men yelling at us.

'Oh good,' said Samson, 'a fight. Come on.'

He took his gate and ran down the hill with it. I made a feeble effort to drag mine then let it drop on the ground and followed him at a distance. He hurled the gate at the three men but thankfully his aim was off, and it sailed over their heads. The men ducked and as they did so he piled into them and sent them sprawling backwards. He picked up the biggest of the three and held him above his head. As the other two scrambled up he hurled the man at them and this time he struck his target. There was the sound of cracking bones and bruising flesh as the three men smashed into one another. Other shouts sounded as more men piled out of houses to join the fray. Samson rubbed his hands, winked at me and ran at a gang of five. There was much cursing and swearing as he threw punches and flung his feet at them. The men scattered with cuts and bruises to show for their trouble. I didn't do anything to help, but then, he didn't need me. He was in his element. Then I felt a hand grab my shoulder and someone spun me round and planted their fist on the right of my jaw. I fell back and stumbled in the dirt. Someone hurled a handful of stones at me and the missiles stung my face and neck. Two bodies piled into mine, one of them held my arms back whilst the other threw punches at my stomach. Then a growl cut through my groans and suddenly the two men were gone, their heads cracked together in Samson's fists. It was a sickening sound. They dropped unconscious. I turned away and threw up. I was wiping my chin when I felt another hand grab me. This time it was him, Samson, and he picked me up and tore up the hill with me, away from the town and out through the ragged remains of the town gates. He laughed as we went and I had the feeling this was his idea of the perfect night out. I just felt ill. Could this man really be a prophet of any kind? A fist-fighting, cavorting philanderer? How could God make any use of someone so patently unholy? Weren't God's people the good ones? The nice guys? Samson was anything but. Spoilt, anarchic, selfish, impetuous. I didn't get it. I really didn't.

He carried me back to a small house in a nearby town, a modest place. He kicked open the door, climbed a ladder to the roof and the next thing I knew he was snoring his head off. I stood in the room below, twiddling my thumbs and doing my best to look inconspicuous. An old man appeared. A version of Samson without the flowing locks, rippling muscles and bad attitude. He smiled at me.

'Good night out was it?' he said.

'Er... sort of. I'm sorry to invade like this. He just brought me home.'

The man flapped a hand at me. 'Don't say a word. We're used to it. I'm his father, Manoah. Would you like some soup, or a drink?' He rubbed at his stubbly chin. 'We don't have wine I'm afraid. Sam's a Nazirite. Totally dedicated to God since birth. No alcohol and no haircuts. It's the way. The angel told us.'

There were a dozen things I didn't comprehend about his little speech, so many things that didn't add up, but I let it rest for now.

He poured some broth into a bowl and handed it to me. I sat at a table and sipped at it. He sat opposite. Samson continued snoring with all the subtlety of a jackhammer. We ignored it.

'He didn't drink anything did he, you know, wine or anything? I'm always worried. He has a habit of being reckless. I think it's all the spirit he has in him. Sets him off like a runaway train sometimes.'

I couldn't resist any longer. I asked him about the angel.

'Oh well, we couldn't have children,' Manoah said,

prizing a sizeable splinter from the table and using it to pick bits of meat from his teeth. 'Thought it was never going to be, but my wife saw an angel one day and he told her she was going to have a son and he'd be totally dedicated to God. I wasn't with her so she told me and I prayed for a sign, I prayed that this man of God would show up again. You see we didn't realise it was an angel at first, just thought it was a prophet or something. Anyway he came back and told me about the no alcohol and haircutting rules and I said I'd get him some food. He wouldn't eat but told us instead to make it an offering to God.' He puffed out his cheeks and his eyebrows slipped upwards at the memory. 'Well! We put the food on a fire and as the flames rose up to heaven – so did the man of God! Couldn't believe it. I promise you as we watched he floated up in the flames. Never seen anything like it.' He shook his head for a while. 'So then we were terrified of course.'

I finished the broth and put the bowl down. Considered his story for a moment. 'Why though?' I asked, 'why terrified?'

'Why? Why? You're asking me why? Because you can't see the presence of God and live. Not if you're a fickle unholy man like me. And angels signify that God's right there with you. So I was convinced we were about to drop dead. I don't know where you're from young man, but round here we respect God. He's almighty and all powerful and when he shows up, we bow.'

'But you didn't die,' I said.

He tapped his nose. 'Very astute. As is my wife. She said the angel wouldn't have bothered going to all that trouble of showing up twice to talk to us about a new baby if God was then going to finish us off. Which was logical as well as wise when you think about it. Bet you never heard anything like it before though eh?' Manoah winked at me. 'An angel turning up to tell a woman she's going to have a baby?'

'Well... er... sort of but... not quite as you describe it...' I fluffed my reply. It was too complicated. 'He seems a fairly impetuous guy your son. Did you know he can rip off a town gate?'

'Oh not that again. We've had that before. It's true he's full of vigour. It's like he's full of spirit but sometimes doesn't demonstrate the restraint. He could do with a few more things like patience, gentleness and self-control. He's a bit short on those. But then he does have a big mission in life.'

'Which is?'

'Getting rid of the Philistines of course. What other big mission could there be in these parts. We need a saviour and he's God's man for the job. One day he'll take them on single-handed and drive them out.'

'By hurling town gates at them?' I said and Manoah laughed.

'Who knows? Might well involve taking apart some bits of architecture. Now would you like a bed, I know it's getting light out there but Sam'll be asleep for another few hours yet.'

I accepted and he gave me a blanket and showed me to a pile of straw in a dark corner. I curled up and let deep sleep take me. But it wouldn't. As I relaxed my mind went into overdrive. I couldn't stop wrestling with all Manoah had told me. An angel appears twice, not just once, but twice to announce this birth. And then the boy turns out to be a renegade terminator. Could that be right? Had the plan gone wrong? It seemed like Samson was missing half the picture, he had the power of God's Spirit without the necessary restraint to channel it. He was like a toddler driving a steamroller. Another Ehud, but a highly unreasonable one. I suppose it was possible, to be anointed for a job but pursue your own agenda. I was no historian but it didn't take much guessing to figure that the past was littered with that kind of thing.

Other images crowded the small space in my head. Images of my recent encounters collided in my brain and did battle in my mind. Ehud with his clever left-handed killing, Noah and his population slaughtering flood, the spies promising Rahab she'd be delivered when the rest of the town was attacked. Ah Rahab. Rahab, Rahab, Rahab. I pictured her face again, remembered that stolen time. Those endless moments when she'd been talking and I'd heard nothing. Just been looking, looking, looking. Drinking in that view. I shook my head, tore myself away. Went back to

Noah, Samson and Ehud. We'd broken into a dangerous world here. If I'd come in looking for light relief I was onto a hiding to nothing. Scheme after scheme concocted to overthrow enemies. Perhaps life had always been violent. Did aggressive times sometimes demand an aggressive response? Ehud and Samson would no doubt have said so. Not Shiphrah and Puah though. And the sight of Noah on his knees trickled onto my mind, praying peaceably whilst the two war-painted tribes did battle around him. Daniel too, resorting to prayer rather than lion-taming. Then there was the likes of Esther, privileged but frightened, and laying her life on the line for others; and impoverished Ruth laying her life on the line for Naomi. Youthful Joe forced by his vengeful brothers to lay his life on the line for his dream. Abigail rescuing David and Nabal. Sarah, Ezekiel, Gideon, Jael, Jeremiah… the visions came and went as I drifted in and out of shallow sleep. So many personalities, so many actors on this huge stage, adlibbing and improvising as they, like me, found themselves in this massive script. This colossal screenplay littered with its heroes and villains, selfish chancers and goodhearted philanthropists. All different personalities, with their own strengths, foibles and weaknesses. None of them the same, no single mould for these Good Book people. It was heartening for a reluctant like me. I'd kinda worried that I might feel an outsider in this place. That I'd stick out like a sore thumb.

Yet I still felt self-conscious. The more the thoughts squabbled with one another and the recent memories fought their battles in my mind, the more sleep slipped away. I was just getting a headache. Eventually I could take it no more and I got up, slipped out of the door and walked for a long time.

25. Jonah

And then I ran for even longer. Stopping at times when I ran out of puff, then picking up speed again as my energy returned. I just wanted to get out of this place. Out of this book. It had given me a headache. Though it sounded madness to think like that even as I was thinking it and desperate to do it. I was so deep in thought and so desperate that I didn't notice the hole in the ground till it swallowed me up. I landed at the bottom of some stone steps. Steps that looked incredibly out of place. Technicolor graffiti lined the stone walls and a guy with creamy dreadlocks and a dirty caftan was strumming a guitar. The tune had a good groove to it and as I got nearer he threw in some words.

I ran for a long time and boarded a boat
I'd get on anything that looked like it could float
I wanted to get away from the call of God
The call to go to Nineveh was dangerous and odd.

His voice was a mix between Bob Dylan and Tracey Chapman, which was unusual to say the least. But the sound was good and he acknowledged me with a nod as I slowed up to listen. I felt obliged then to hang around. I looked for a hat full of coins on the ground but there was nothing.

So I got on this boat and I sailed the other way
Then a storm blew up at the height of the day
I was fast asleep but the crew woke me up
And when they told me about it I knew what was up.

The storm wasn't normal - it was plain divine
I knew I had to put my life on the line
So I told them 'Throw me over and I'll see you around'
And they hurled me in the waves and I fell down, down.

Then the strangest thing, a fish came along
And this is the weirdest part of the song
Many folks claim that I made it up
But I kid you not the fish swallowed me up.

Inside the beast was no game of skittles
So I got on my knees amongst the food and the spittle
And I talked to God and I changed my mind
And I told him my life was right there on the line.

So the whale got sick and he felt real sore
And he threw me up on Nineveh's shore
I walked around preaching and covered in vomit
And those Ninevites sure got the message from it.

They prayed and fasted and laid their lives on the line
And God took a look and changed his mind
He didn't want to kill them, he wanted them back
And I felt like I'd been stabbed in the back.

I knew he'd turn around and forgive those folk
After I'd walked round looking like one big joke
Being a prophet ain't the kind of life you'd wish
There are days when I'd rather just be a big fish.

So I found some shade from the heat of the day
And would you know it – the shade withered away
I was mad with God for letting me fry
And I told him he'd better just let me die.

But he answered me back after not too long
Told me I'd got my priorities wrong
The loss of one plant had filled me with pity
But God cared about these people in the city.

That's about the end of this really strange tale.
You may know it as Jonah and the whale
It'll be round forever to tell the people all
Not to be surprised when God gives a call.
Not to be surprised when God gives a call.
Not to run away when God gives a call...

He went back to strumming the tune. I felt in my
pockets for a couple of coins and laid a few in a little
stack in front of him. He'd shut his eyes now and
wasn't watching. I waited to see if he'd spot my
generosity but there was nothing from him. So then I
wondered about picking up the coins again as he
didn't seem bothered, but I heard footsteps coming
and realised I couldn't be seen stealing a busker's

wage. I moved on quickly, breaking into a run as the words of the song rattled around the backstage of my mind.

Not to run away…
Not to run away…
Not to run away…
The words kept pounding in my brain as the blood began thundering round my head, the pressure building with every step I took. Like a car alarm that keeps invading your space no matter how far away you move from it.
Not to run away…

I was running all right, no doubt about that, but I had no idea which way the running was taking me. Maybe I'd find a boat to Nineveh waiting for me somewhere. I went on through the tunnel, brushing against the concrete and the graffiti. The blood went on pumping round my head and my lungs grew short of oxygen. The tunnel went on forever, no let up, I just wanted some daylight now. My head swam a little and suddenly that damn dream reared its head again.

I'm lying by the road, off my head after another night out, as ever abandoned by my so-called friends, and yes, here we go again, I grab at my pockets and discover the scabs have run off with my cash. My wallet's here but never more empty. They'll laugh about it tomorrow as we shift stuff in the factory, but it's no joke to me. Happens too often. Me left nursing the old headache and short of cash to see me through the week yet again. I hear a step and know that for once one of them has come back for me, maybe to help me up, maybe to apologise, maybe to give me at least my bus fare home. But the hand reaching for me doesn't go for my arm, it goes for my face instead. Slapping me hard, and again. A third time and I'm seeing stars. I feel a boot in my ribs and smell urine and mud on the leather. I tuck my head under my arms and hug the floor as the fists rain down on me. In my head I go somewhere else, a safe place, another world where these things don't happen. But the beating and the spitting and the cursing goes on.

On.

And on.

And on…

…time passes. I'm getting cold. They took my jacket and I don't know where they threw it. The pain in my ribs is getting worse. As I start to shiver it's a nightmare. More time goes. I start to fade into some other reality. I don't hear the steps, just feel a hand shaking me. I look up. An old guy frowns then smiles at me…

Daylight. I blundered up the steps and outside. And suddenly the desert was gone. I was on a railway station. No sign of any boats to Nineveh. That was a relief. But the change of scene was completely disorientating. That coupled with how conflicted I now felt after my encounter with Samson, and the whole thing just left me dizzy and sick. I wanted out.

No more wandering and meeting people. I needed help now. I'd ventured into the Good Book and it had left me battered. I threw a silent prayer towards the heavens and looked around for some help.

Part Two
The Stations

1. Aladdin and Isabeth

The station was deserted. Not even a woman in the ticket office or a disgruntled station attendant. A few bits of litter kicked up against the walls. Then a distant figure appeared on a far bench, I could have sworn she was the woman in white. But she no sooner sat down than she changed her mind and stood up to leave. From nowhere, with no warning, a train rounded the bend and pulled in, bringing with it a cloud of smoke and steam. And a strange smell about it too. The carriages were blood red and the outer paintwork scarred. A door stopped right in front of me. I looked back for the woman in white but she'd gone. I got on.

The carriage had a corridor running alongside the trail of compartments. Most were empty, a few had one or two folks sitting inside. The full gamut of travellers from the jokers, laughers and chatterers, through to the lonely ones, some staring into space, some reading, one or two looking terrified or sad. But all in all, the train was far from full. There was a lurch that threw me further along the corridor and the train started up. I landed beside the final compartment. And blow me down Aladdin was in there. Along with the sandwich maker's niece. Her name eluded me when I first spotted her there, all calm and sharp and neat. She and Aladdin were nattering about something. Aladdin as ever was animated and cheerful. She was having none of it. Sat like a statue, still, straight-backed and immovable, just occasionally pursing those lips of hers and giving the slightest nod of her head. If I'd have been Aladdin I'd have been cowed into submission, abandoning any urge towards animation in order to conform to her rigor mortis mode of operating. But Aladdin was Aladdin. Oozing life and optimism, and intent on gathering her up into his world of wonder. I stood watching them, not quite believing it. Finally I had found them. Perhaps we were going home.

Aladdin wore denims most of the time. Jeans with snags and rips and inky graffiti on them. Plus a jacket with the sleeves missing over a t-shirt with some film reference. The night we met the sandwich maker he had a Jaws poster regaling his chest. That ominous great white shark rising from the depths like a deadly, aquatic killing machine, lunging for his neck. In spite of Aladdin's downbeat appearance there was always a cool thing about him, a kind of ragged optimism, rogue sophistication even. And he always smelt great. I have a keen sense of smell. She smelt good too. I noticed when I slid open the door. Isabeth. Her name came back to me as soon as I entered the carriage. I was so happy to see them. So relieved I nearly collapsed. I wanted to hug them both, but it's not in my nature. They looked at me at first as if I was an intruder. Then Aladdin's face lit up and Isabeth raised her sharp, neat eyebrows in recognition.

'Where've you been?' Aladdin chirped, half getting up.

'We thought you may have bottled out,' Isabeth said quietly.

'How could I bottle out?' I said, 'I drank the same green smoking stuff you did. I plugged into the same wires.'

Aladdin sat back down and looked me up and down.

'What happened to you?' he said.

They both looked me up and down. The rips in my clothes, the stains, the creases and sweat marks, the spatters of blood and a single spray of vomit. And all this in spite of my many attempts to get clean. This was going to take a little time.

'I'm hungry,' I said. 'This train carry any food?'

'Nope.'

I went to sit down beside Isabeth but Aladdin's face told me, 'No! Don't do that!'

I glanced down at myself again and then at her with her smart, clean, never-been-creased grey suit and I got it. I sat on Aladdin's side, as far away from him as possible. I guess I must have smelt bad too. That's the funny thing about smell, you might have a keen sense but you never much pick up your own. Familiarity I suppose.

'I fell down a well,' I said.

'You drowned?' Aladdin said, his eyes wide.

I gave him an ironic stare. 'Yea, I drowned, that's how I'm here taking to you.'

'Well you mighta done, we're here riding a train inside the pages of a book. What could be impossible?'

'I didn't drown, Al, but I did land on someone.'

'Ouch!'

I looked at Isabeth as she said this, she didn't look like she'd ever fallen down anything in her life. And yet I couldn't help thinking that she'd cope whatever came her way. No doubt looking pristine wherever she landed.

'This dude was already down there. Sitting in the dark, fuming and licking his wounds. Literally. He looked a little bit mad, his eyes wide and bulging and he was singing this song about how he felt like he'd been beaten up by a bear.'

'A bear? Down a well?' Isabeth looked momentarily startled. She was finally beginning to show a little emotion here.

'Well no, there was no bear down there, but he'd been knocked about by the guys who threw him in the well and as he'd only been doing what he thought God wanted him to do it felt as if the big man had mauled him about like a bear might do. There was another body down there – we thought it might be you, Al.'

'Oh great! Thanks,' said Aladdin, then, 'Hey! What was the song? D'it have a good vibe?'

'Mournful,' I said, 'more like *Hotel California* than *Jailhouse Rock*.'

'That's cool,' Aladdin said, grimacing and nodding.

I wanted to say more, about the stresses and terrors of the last twenty-four hours. About aiding and abetting the murder of Eglon, and failing to rescue Joe, about falling for Rahab and getting caught in a rock fight with Noah and his neighbours. Standing there in that carriage I knew then just how much it had taken out of me. Part of me, a small part of me, wanted to be a kind of hero, but the bigger part wanted to go home. I wasn't made for this. I wanted out. But I said nothing more, because I knew they wouldn't understand, and more than that, I was scared that Isabeth would be disapproving and Aladdin disappointed in me.

I looked around. 'Where's the old man?' I asked.

'You mean my uncle?' Isabeth asked, skewing her head a little.

'Yea, the magic man. The one who got us into this.'

She cleared her throat. 'Well, first off, we all got ourselves into this. And second, this is not magic.'

The train slowed then speeded up again and Aladdin and I lurched forward. Not Isabeth, barely a shoulder twitch from her. I pulled out my moleskine notebook and began scribbling, my writing, as ever, was barely legible to even me.

'What are you writing?' Isabeth asked.

'Thought I'd make a few notes, I figure that

trekking across the inside of a bestseller might provide some good material for the inside of another bestseller.'

'Is that ethical?' she asked.

'Ethical?' Al and I said this together, though I was a little slower and my last syllable dragged and finished after his.

'Yes,' she cleared her throat, 'making money out of something already published by someone else.'

I squinted at Al, he squinted back. Then he grinned.

'Doubt it,' he said, 'but in the end everything's plagiarism isn't it? 99% of what we say is just clichés that someone else has already said.'

'All original ideas are really just combinations of previously concocted notions,' I added, an argument I'd used many times before, though it sounded hollow when I was looking at Isabeth Constana.

Silence.

As I did my best to scribble snapshots of the many recent encounters, my head span with the memory of them all. 'So many,' I muttered to myself. 'So many characters, coming thick and fast. And furious.'

Isabeth heard me. 'That's the Bible for you,' she said.

'Why do you think the dress is all wrong?' I asked.
'The dress? What dress?' said Al, standing up, sliding open the top window and sticking his head through it so that the last part of 'dress' got lost in the rush of air.

'Everyone's dress. I mean, I'm no biblical historian but Ezekiel was wearing blue baggy trousers and a yellow flowery shirt.'

Al stuck his head back in, thought for a moment, then said, 'Maybe he did wear that.'

'I doubt it,' said Isabeth, in her cold quiet kind of way.

Silence. I scribbled.

'And the timing of things seems askew,' I said. 'The order of events, you know? Random. And this train. Who said there was a railway in the Bible?'

'I believe our imagination plays a chief part in the way things work here,' she said. 'Part of what we experience is in the book, part is in our mind.'

'Hmm, which I guess is the way it works when we read anything anyway,' I muttered.

She raised an eyebrow. 'Profound,' she said, and she pursed her lips.

'So,' I said, on a roll now and jabbing my stubby pencil towards her, 'what we're experiencing now is really just an extension of reading. Like flipping back and forward through a book. Reading various bits.'

She smiled, said nothing and nodded. Then the smile disappeared. Smiling transformed her face. Perhaps that's why she was cautious about doing it. I wished she did it more.

Silence. I scribbled again.

'So…' I swivelled my pencil in a circle, pointing to the three of us, 'who's mind conjured up the train?'

'I doubt that matters,' said Isabeth.

Al pulled his head in again, his hair was getting out of control now and there were flies sticking to his face. 'I love trains,' he announced. Then he poked his head outside again.

I raised my eyebrows and jabbed my pencil towards him. Isabeth said nothing. I watched the passing greeny blue blur, and scribbled from time to time. Isabeth closed her eyes and sighed. She leant back against the seat.

'I read Bible stories growing up,' I said, 'and went to Sunday school. But it's been a while.'

Isabeth nodded and merely said, 'You know more than you think.' Then she adjusted her back against the seat, her eyes still closed. I heard Al whooping out of the window into the mad rush of air.

2. The Inbetween

'Where are we going?' I asked.

Al pulled his head in, his hair now extraordinarily wild from the battering of air outside.

'No idea,' he said and added, 'I like that.'

'You like what?' I said.

'Being on the road to anywhere. Didn't Talking Heads sing about that?'

'No,' I said, 'they were on the road to nowhere.'

'Oh we're definitely not that,' Al said with a huge grin.

He stuck his head back out and let out a yelp of happiness.

'Where's the sandwich maker? We need to find him,' I said.

'I don't know,' said Isabeth, her eyes still closed behind her sharp silver glasses. 'But I do have the feeling we should find him if we want to be out of here.'

'Who wants to get out of here?' Al yelped, pulling his head back in. 'We only just got here.'

And he shoved his head straight back outside again.

'Clearly, Aladdin is here for an adventure,' Isabeth said, opening one eye now. 'What are you here for?'

I wasn't sure. Why not be here? Everyone has to be somewhere. Who said that? Can't recall, a comedian I think.

'Mad Dan Eccles,' I said aloud.

That ruffled her feathers, at long last. Both eyes burst wide and she leant forward. She broke the rigid stance of her stiff upper body and said, 'What?'

I laughed. 'Oh, just thinking aloud, he said something once. Spike Milligan I believe. *Everyone's gotta be somewhere.*'

She resumed her posture, raised an eyebrow, and pursed those lips. 'Really?' she said. 'That's why you're here? I don't believe you.'

I didn't believe me either. I thought I'd got away with it, that 'accidental' outburst, that weird *Goons* quote. I thought it would take us off into the realms of great quotes and memorable wisdom.

She stared me out and waited. I crumbled.

'I guess I'm bored. Frustrated. Want more. For a moment back there, in reality, when Al told me about your hazy crazy uncle's idea, well I figured I had nothing to lose. Didn't much expect it to work anyway, but if it could work, why not go to another place, a different world? Scientists are spending millions on trying to Mars-walk aren't they? Look at us – Mars-walking inside a paperback. Who'd'a thought that? So why wouldn't I say yes to a ride like this?'

'Hmm,' she glanced away, out of the window. I could tell she didn't swallow it. But she was wrong. It had to be half the truth, I just wasn't sure of the other half. Why was anybody dissatisfied with life if you had a half decent existence? Why kick against the goads if things were even marginally hunky dory? I sighed inwardly. Why had I done it? Why? The answers seemed too complicated for me to unravel. And I wasn't going to make any mention of the bridge, of course.

'What about you?' I asked.

She continued staring out of the window for a while, eventually tearing her gaze away from the blurry view in slow motion, as if she was looking at the eighth wonder of the world and didn't want to miss a single split second. She looked at me long and hard, unflinching, unblinking. It was verging on becoming one of those 'who can blink first' games. You can work out who lost.

'As you were saying,' she said eventually, still without blinking, 'we need to find my uncle.'

That was no answer. And we both knew it. She stood up and slipped out into the corridor. A single glance back told me I should follow. I looked at Al, he was still having the time of his life, his head stuck out into the raging stream of air.

'When I was young my old man…' she coughed, 'my father, was highly organised. He hated mess. I remember one day he came downstairs and found the kitchen in a mess after I'd been trying my hand at making cakes. He blew his top. Threw a few bits of crockery and a couple of pans. Which of course made more mess.' She looked at me over the top of her glasses, for the first time I spotted a spark of fear in those cool blue eyes. 'He never laid a hand on me or my sister or my mother. He wasn't that sort of man. But he was obsessive about this tidiness issue. So I learnt to follow his lead and keep him happy. I caught the obsessive virus I suppose. But what you see on the surface is never the full picture is it, no matter how much someone appears to be "what you see is what you get." Everyone has their shadows and secrets.'

I cleared my throat and looked away for a moment.

She went on. 'When he died my sister and I went through his study. My mother couldn't face doing it. We found a bureau stuffed with papers going back decades, unsorted, some of it scrunched up like litter. He'd just kept pushing it in there, keeping his mess out of the way. The bottom drawer contained something green that was probably an old sandwich he'd shoved away a long time before. It was disgusting.' She paused for a moment and looked out of the window. 'Be nice not to worry about order for a while.' She looked into the compartment, at the back of Al's head. 'I envy Aladdin. He seems so carefree. That would be nice.'

My father had been a quiet man. Loved painting model soldiers and collecting old 45s. Everything from Elvis, Frank and Dusty, to Bernard Cribbins and The Who. Not Bernard Cribbins *and* The Who. As far as I know Pete and Roger never shared a mic with Bernard. He was a true gentleman really, my father.

Always kind to my mother and never let a coarse word trip across his lips. But the house had been quiet too, not a sociable hive of improvised meals for guests dropping by, or a haven of hastily made beds for friends unexpectedly in the neighbourhood. We had lived quietly (apart from the noisier 45s) and the experience shaped me. Crafted me into the kind of guy who was happy with less people around.

'I've always loved my uncle,' Isabeth was saying, dragging me from my reverie. 'He's an inventor you know. A genius really. He trained as a priest, but tried it and caved in under the pressure. He wasn't thick-skinned enough. You have to be prepared to take a lot of flak and he couldn't. So he took up teaching science instead, while all the time his real passion was inventing things. When he got tired of teaching – too much flak again – he opened up the sandwich bar with the film theme. Movies and sandwiches come a close second and third for him, after inventing. He used to have this laboratory in his garage. It was a big old building with huge wooden doors, covered in red paint that was peeling off. I remember being fascinated by this smaller doorway we went through, cut into the much bigger doors. It felt as if we were going into another world. A secret, mysterious world. He never kept his car in there. Instead it was full of bicycle wheels and bits of old Meccano sets and brightly coloured wires. He once made a flying machine for an injured robin. And water wings for a reluctant duck. Seriously. No cruelty involved, he only did it to help. He adores animals. He said he was looking forward to meeting a talking donkey on this trip. Was there a talking donkey? Did you meet a talking donkey?'

Oh I met a talking donkey all right.

'Well, I hope he did, like I say, he adores animals. Where was I? Oh yes. Inventions. He also claimed he'd invented a transporter, you know Star Trek style. It was wrapped in chains and under a sheet of canvas in a dark corner, so I never saw it. I begged him to show it to me but he wouldn't, said he'd let me try out another invention he was working on. It turned out to be this. He'd been tinkering with this one for a long time.' She paused and reflected, then went on. 'He's always treated me like a friend you know, even when I was little, like I was an equal. Never talked down to me, always loved sharing his new ideas. A kind man, a very kind man. Such a friend. He got me through some hard times. Sometimes I'd go in his lab, fed up after another day at school, and he'd just let me sit there and watch him making something. No questions, no advice. He just let me be. A great guy. Mad, but great.'

The train slowed a little and the blurry images outside came into focus. Work teams were digging roads out there, gangs of labourers commandeered by Roman soldiers. Officers on horses patrolled the soldiers patrolling the workers. There was sweat everywhere.

'Who are they?' I asked.

'Don't you recognise the rise of the Roman Empire when you see it?' she said.

'I've never watched it from a train window before.'

'I believe we're currently in the 400 years,' she said.

'What 400 years?'

'Between the Testaments. The 400 year gap. The in-between. You know it?'

I shook my head and leant wearily against the glass. Outside whips were being wielded as the labourers struggled to keep up with their quotas. A crack sounded and a couple of trails of blood dotted the window right in front of my face. I recoiled.

'The silent gap. No words from God. No sacred writing. The waiting.'

'What for?' I traced the lines of blood with my finger. They were spreading into a strangely shaped smear, pulled about by the rushing wind outside.

I glanced at Isabeth, she had taken out a mirror and was fixing her make up.

'The world to change dramatically,' she answered. 'The coming of Alexander the Great and the rise of the Roman Empire. The young Macedonian had a vision. A single language for the whole world.'

'I thought that was English,' I said.

She forced a smile. 'Greek. Changed everything. Big Alex conquered the world with his words. Then the Romans pitched up with their roads and lines of communication and the world was a radically different place. By the time the New Testament kicked in the world was vastly different. Global communication was born. Long before the internet.'

'Why did that matter?'

The blood had formed into a ragged cross on the glass.

'Why d'you think?' she said, pencilling a line under her eye.

I ran my finger over the bloody pattern.

'I think I have an idea,' I said.

She looked up at me, then at the window.

'Aha,' was all she said.

In the distance a colossal bridge was emerging from the earth as construction crews swarmed over it like ants on a discarded, half-eaten lump of cake. Whips cracked there too but I could only see the flick of the lashes, any sound was never going to travel this far. The train picked up speed and the builders and soldiers blurred into a misty grey and red montage. We went back into the compartment. Al pulled his head in and whistled.

'Man those Romans were efficient, eh?' he said, wiping dark grit and tiny red specks from his face.

Isabeth cleared her throat and spoke again.

She said, 'I believe this train is following the Hodos Paradeisō. The way to paradise.'

Al grinned and punched the air. 'Yes, we're following in the steps of the three seers.'

'Four seers,' Isabeth said, quietly.

'How d'you know where we're going?' I said.

She put her make-up away. Didn't rush her reply. 'I spoke to the driver earlier. I requested it.'

'You can do that?'

She replaced her glasses and adjusted the frame a little, lifted the weight of them off her face for a split-second. 'Apparently so. I got the impression it might take a while.'

As she said this the train slowed again and a station slid into view. A huge crimson number 1 was suspended on a solid black cable from the roof. The train stopped. I went out into the corridor and unlatched the door. I heard steps behind me. Al was looking out of the door.

'Can we get off?' I asked.

'Do what you like, mate,' he said with a grin.

I got off.

3. The Creature

I felt him before I saw him. I presume he was a 'he'. You can't really tell with huge great towering creatures with scales and smoking breath. The ground shook as I left the station and started walking down a deserted high street. The shops were all boarded up and I figured everyone must have known something I didn't. I clearly missed that memo. The ground shook again and then I heard the roar. Seconds later I heard a baby crying, coming from above one of the boarded-up stores. I shivered, then wondered why as the air was warm. Warm and getting warmer with every tremble of the ground. I turned and saw nothing. The street was still bare, bits of litter kicking up against each other. I stood still and waited. Another roar. Then a hiss, a quiet breathy sound. I looked to my left and right, then back to my right and above me. A woman's face, creased with stress. And her hand waving towards me out of an apartment window.

'Here,' she said, 'up here.'

I took that as an invitation and made for the door below. It was covered with posters for old concerts, defaced and peeling off, hanging there like bits of skin off a suntan gone wrong. I tried the handle, it was loose and turned and I went in. The shop was dark and empty and it didn't smell; good. Over in the corner I spotted the stairs and took them two at a time. She met me at the top. A young woman, maybe only fifteen or so, with the crying baby clutched to her small body. She was no bigger than Miriam but I figured this teenager was not the baby's sister. Things hit you at the strangest moments sometimes, and it was at this moment that I realised I'd lost Al and Isabeth again. I'd been so relieved to see them on that train and now here I was alone again. My saviours are back there somewhere sitting in a safe carriage. Great. The roar came again.

'We have to get out of here,' she said. 'We have to get to safety.'

'And where's that?' I asked.

She shrugged. Her face was so innocent beyond the stress. Her eyes wide and her features soft and unblemished. She shouldn't have been here with me in a derelict building, she should have been in an advert for something that promised to make life better. She handed me the bundle that continued to cry, in fact it went to screaming pitch as it entered my arms.

'Look,' she said, speaking up over the noise, 'I was given these.'

She held up a crystal bottle of perfume, branded with a number one logo, a small gold casket, encrusted with tiny jewels, and a bundle of money. The perfume alone was worth a small fortune.

'Where did you get all these?' I said, doing my best to rock some silence into the baby.

She smiled. 'Gifts,' she said. 'We can buy our way

out.'

'Out of where?'

'This place. We need to escape and we'll need food. Plus it takes money to bribe border guards.'

She suddenly looked a whole lot less innocent. The building trembled again and it was followed by another roar, like thunder following a streak of lightning. She shoved the gifts into a canvas shoulder bag, gave it to me, swapping it for her baby and she led me to a door in the far wall. I did my best to shove it open but it wasn't moving. She pushed me aside and patted it softly three times. It swung wide. She looked at me and raised her petite eyebrows, then disappeared down the narrow stairwell beyond. I followed. The steps went beyond ground level and deep under the street. They emerged into a damp tunnel. She seemed to know where she was going so I just played catchup. Rats scattered as we ran and dark insects flitted across the walls, but underground there was no sound of the roaring or any shivers from the shaking ground above. I figured we were getting away. Then the tunnel came to an end. She brushed cockroaches from the black smeary handle above her head, twisted it and pushed. Daylight crept in as she handed me the baby. He was quieter now, lying there studying my face with a furrowed brow. I'd say he looked a lot like her, but then that's what people say anyway. She climbed up and reached back down to me. I handed her the child and the bag and hoiked myself up and through the hole.

I had figured wrong. The ground shook as soon as I put my feet on it and the loudest roar in the world shook everything. I turned and my guts felt like water. There in the distance, a fiery red and with more heads than anything I'd ever seen before – I kid you not – was this massive dragon. No wonder the roaring was so loud, it was coming from seven yawning chasm mouths.

'We're dead,' I said.

'Shut up,' she replied and she pointed the other way.

We ran. Through empty streets, heading step by step away from civilisation and towards the wilderness. The road turned potholed and then began to fade and become a rough track. I wondered how far away the train was now. The train and Al and safety. Would I ever get back there? Could you break into the Good Book and die from dragon bites? We ran on. Somewhere behind us there was more roaring and the sound of crumbling masonry. I looked back. The dragon was swinging its various heads into the buildings behind us, three or four at a time. Windows fell in, walls spilt onto the street like discarded Lego, and furniture and plumbing spewed from the open wounds. Ambivalent to the damage it was causing the creature kept coming, crushing the debris with its boulder feet as it went. He was gaining on us. Up ahead I could see a huge figure looming. As we closed in I could make out the colour of grey stone. The thing was a giant statue. Then, I swear, it moved. It turned its head and blinked its stone grey eyes at us. What on earth was this place? We gave it a wide berth as it opened its mouth and started to speak. Something about a call to worship. The girl ignored it and pointed towards a gatehouse.

'The border,' she said.

It didn't look much considering it was going to save us from a seven-headed dragon and a talking statue. A couple of soldiers came out as we approached.

'Passes,' they said.

Behind us the statue called again. They took no notice of it. Then the ground shook and I looked back to see the creature still coming.

'We don't have passes,' she said.

They began to argue then she held up a hand.

'We have money though,' she said.

They shut up. She pulled out a small bundle of notes, much smaller than the one she'd shown me. She held them out. The guards, both red-eyed and blotchy faced, reached for them. The broader one slapped the other's hand away and took the money. He made a big show of licking his fingers and counting them with a wet, broken-nailed thumb.

'Not enough,' he said with a leery grin, and he looked the girl up and down.

I stepped between them. 'It has to be enough,' I said.

Both soldiers laughed. A sneering, 'you don't know who you're messing with' kind of laugh.

'Take him out back,' the stocky guy snapped, and the other one slapped a grimy, hairy hand on my arm.

I pulled free, but he grabbed me again, just as an ear-splitting roar cut the air. The ground was all tremors as we turned to look. The creature with the heads was only twenty paces away. Twenty of our paces, not his. He'd be on us in a single smoky breath. Somewhere behind him the statue called again about worship. The soldiers shouldered their guns and without taking much aim started firing. Bullets pinged off the dragon like frozen peas from a plastic shooter. One head flinched as a better shot caught it in the eye. A trickle of strange blood ran down its rocky face and the dragon halted for a moment, roared in pain, then lunged right at us. We scattered. I went one way, the girl the other. The fighters, to their credit, stood their ground in the middle. More bullets flew and rebounded. One of them hit the dirt at my feet, sending up a shower of grit. Two of the dragon's heads fell on the men like the scoops on giant earth movers. The men let out screams that were quickly swallowed up along with them. A few bits of gore fell on the road, along with their clattering rifles. I stopped running to look for the girl and her baby. She was hurtling across the border, in the gap left by the two grey-uniformed guards. I started after her. A sudden hand came from nowhere, gripped my shoulder and with extraordinary strength pulled me so far back I nearly fell sprawling. I steadied myself and looked around, it was the woman in white, clearly stronger than I'd ever imagined.

'What are you doing?' I gasped at her.

'Stopping you, if you go any further you'll be in serious danger,' she said.

'Serious danger? what d'you think I've been in for the last hour?'

'They'll be fine, your job is done.'

'What job?'

'Looking after them.'

'I didn't do anything.'

She smiled. 'Yes you did. Look.'

She pointed, a second figure ran across the border to the mother and child. They hugged hurriedly.

'Joe, the husband,' she said, 'they'll escape now.'

We stood watching as the three small figures melted away from us. The creature took a look at the woman in white and twisted its seven heads away from us. He lumbered away back towards the statue who called out yet again.

'Can I go home, I've had enough,' I said to the woman.

She shrugged. 'Soon,' she said and she sounded exactly like a mother trying to convince a child everything would be fine.

4. The Stranger

At that moment I felt as if I could sleep forever. All the energy fled my body and my knees buckled. The woman in white grabbed me, hooked her arm under mine and led me away from the scene. I shut my eyes and my head swam. Right then, at that moment, I didn't care if I lived or died. Let the dragon take me and split me seven ways. It wasn't courage. Just exhaustion. The woman walked me for a while, struggling to keep herself upright under my weight. We must have looked like a weary, drunken couple. Then she let me slump down, patted my shoulder and let me go. I heard her steps fading away. And then I heard the train. I opened my eyes. I could have cried. I was on another railway station, and here came the train again, in its cloudy, steamy glory. Washing into the station like an ocean of fresh water for a dying man. I stood up, staggered towards it, and grabbed the nearest door. I was on board. Let it take me home. Please.

'You look worse every time I see you.'

It was Isabeth, peering at me over the top of her tidy, silver glasses.

Aladdin pulled his head in from the window, his face was spattered with grime and flies, but he was grinning like mad.

'Not enjoying yourself?' he asked, clearly chuffed to see me again.

'What happened to you guys?' I demanded. 'I got off the train and found myself in a war zone. You two meanwhile sit here like a couple of chirpy little birds, on a happy sunny day.'

It was the only description I could think of as I threw myself onto the seat opposite Isabeth. I was still mindful enough to avoid contaminating her pristine suit.

'Are you two just spending all the time on this train while I do the running about and… and…'

I ran out of words. My mouth flapped but nothing would come. So I changed tactics and sobbed. I gave in and looked the fool. How could anyone understand? How would they ever believe what I'd just experienced? I was cornered. Exhausted by the trauma and totally alone with the experience. I shoved my face in my hands and that was when I felt a movement next to me. I smelt her as she put a hand around my shoulder. Isabeth. Right there next to me, getting grubby as she tried to encourage me. I said nothing. We sat like that for a while. Quite a while.

'When you battle with the dragon it leaves you empty sometimes,' she said quietly.

I looked up. Al was standing watching us, not sure what to make of this.

'The dragon?' I said and she nodded.

'You're bound to be wrung out,' she said. 'Sometimes the fighting is subtle. But not today. Not for you.'

How did she know?

'I'll get you a coffee,' she said, and she stood up.

'Do they have coffee on this train?' I asked and she laughed one of her rare laughs.

'If we want it,' she said and she slid the door open behind her. She lingered for a moment and studied me with her cool, blue eyes, then she turned and went.

I followed her out into the corridor and watched the world rushing by. This strange, sacred, literary kingdom that none of us should have, by rights, been trekking through. Yet here we were and there it was, right outside the train window, racing past. The train suddenly slowed at that moment and the blurry bits of scene outside gathered together like paint swirling into a haphazard picture. I heard the sound of hammering and men calling out from their various workstations. The train slowed to a crawl, then to a hesitant stop, and I caught sight of a builder and his mate, repairing a roof, on a house that looked as if it had been ravaged by fire. The builder was older, could well have been the younger man's father. They worked with callus-handed precision. Swung hammers at nails as if they'd been doing it all their lives. From time to time one would make a comment and the other laugh. The younger guy bounded around like a young gazelle, his feet adapting to the crooks and crevices of the wounded building. He wiped sweat from his brow and his grinning top lip as he worked, pushing hair from his eyes whenever it clouded his view. Then the sound of hooves straightened the men's faces. A couple of straight-backed Romans on sweat-sheened horses rode into town. They slowed to a stop as they passed the ravaged house. One of them barked an order to the younger builder. He climbed down in a single bound and fished about amongst the debris below. Then he produced something, a knife perhaps, and held it up, the charred handle towards the Roman. The soldier eyed him for a moment, the teenager's hand hovering in the air. Eventually the soldier spat at his feet and snatched the blade from him. He examined it and nodded. The other soldier sneered and said something to the builders. He took the knife from his colleague, looked at it, sniffed it, scowled and secured it in a sheath. Then they dug their heels into the flesh of their animals, slapped the backs of their necks with the reins and steered them out of town.

For a moment I lifted my gaze beyond the two builders. The town was full of sacked houses, there were builders everywhere, repairing Roman damage I figured. There were dark pools in the street, and bits of clothing and furniture strewn here and there, waiting for the tidying up. There was also the odd fire, flames poking from piles of broken wood. I could imagine the smell of wood smoke and dirt, shavings and sweat. Blood too, possibly, if I was right about the dark pools there. The young builder looked up at his father and said something with a smile. His father, stern and stone-faced throughout the Roman interruption, laughed suddenly He said something in return and offered his hand to pull the young builder up. The train started up again and the town slipped away.

I never got the coffee. The train pulled up again before she returned and Al gave a yell and stuck his head back out of the window. I went to look. The place was a picture. Calm tranquil sea, men in jeans and t-shirts, working contentedly in their boats, the warm sun bouncing off the water and sending its rays towards us. It looked idyllic out there, a scene reeking of peace and order, I felt suddenly calmer. And feeling that way I got the strangest of notions about wanting to get out again. I wanted the coffee too but I figured fresh air wouldn't have the bitter aftertaste, and the drink would still be there when I got back. That's when I spotted the radio. A cheap, yellow transistor sitting on a table by the window. Joan Osborne was singing, her earnest, potent, questioning voice just a small, tinny noise in the background.

She was singing about God, and what name he might have, and whether you'd use it if you met him face to face. She was asking what we'd ask him if we had one question. And what it might be like to see his face. Whether we'd really want to do it. I thought of Manoah, and his dread at having encountered God through an angel. Perhaps, she sang, he was on a bus somewhere, just a stranger, looking like the rest of us, on his way home after another difficult day. Did God have difficult days, I wondered? I couldn't help thinking of those builders. Their day appeared good *and* difficult. Maybe that was close to the truth.

'Coming?' I asked Al, indicating the world beyond the window.

He thought about this. 'Can't both leave without Isabeth,' he said.

I didn't stop to consider this, I was outside and running across the tracks towards the sea.

I slipped into the water and threw two handfuls over my face. It felt good to wash away the tears and the fear and the stark memories. I washed for a while. Eventually I crawled back to the shore and collapsed in the sun. I could hear voices. A couple of boats nearby, two men discussing something in earnest.

'What do you think?' the younger one was saying. The bigger guy, bushy-bearded and stern-faced, shrugged. When he spoke he sounded as if he was in charge.

'I feel indebted,' he said. 'I *am* indebted.'

'You mean your mother-in-law?' said the young, fresh-faced guy, 'How she somehow got better so quick.'

'You don't have to dress it up,' he snapped back, 'he cured her. There's no way she would have been up and about like that without him going to see her.' He rubbed his beard and growled like an impatient dog. 'So as a result I owe him now.'

'But you leant him your boat, the other day. That's payment. He fixed your mother, you helped him out.'

He nodded and rubbed a scarred hand through his beard again. He rubbed hard, as if he was doing his best to shove it off his face. Or if not that, to get rid of some other problem in his life.

'But that's the thing, John,' he said. 'Sitting in that boat, nowhere to go, just sat there listening to him. I've never heard a rabbi teach like that. I tell you, he was something else. And then all those fish. How did he know they were down there?'

John shrugged.

'And why give them to us? Worth a fortune. You see, it leaves me indebted again. We're both indebted. He wants something. He's got me cornered and I can't say no.'

'What d'you mean – cornered?'

'Well, if he comes looking for me I have no excuse. That catch of fish he found – that'll take care of both our families for a good while. I've been thinking about this. We don't need to fish do we, not right now. We have no excuse John.'

'No excuse for what?'

'Refusing him!' the big guy boomed and some of the other men looked over.

A third guy came over, a bigger version of the young guy with a beard to rival the big man.

'He's in town again,' he said, and his voice was rich and resonant. I could imagine him doing documentary voice-overs.

The big guy slapped his hand on the water and a colossal spray doused all three of them.

'Simon! Easy!' said the other bearded guy.

John wiped water from his eyes. 'Well, he ain't here, so we needn't worry,' he said.

Running steps, and a fourth guy came over. Red-faced, wild hair, fire in his eyes. A smile playing on his lips.

'Oh great,' said Simon, 'little brother's happy, that always spells trouble.'

'He's back,' the new guy said, breathlessly, 'and he's headed this way.'

The big fisherman leapt up. 'Come on,' he said.

'Where you going?' John said.

'Where d'you think? Fishing. It's what we do, remember?'

'But I thought you just said…'

'Shut up!'

He pushed his boat out with his little brother and the others pitched in and gave a hand.

'Don't you want to stay around and see him again?' his brother asked.

'Is Caesar Jewish?' Simon muttered back. 'Come on Andrew! Get in!'

The brothers jumped in the boat and began to row out from the shore. John and James stood watching, the water lapping at their legs.

John looked to the skies. 'Storm coming,' he said.

'What?'

'The weather James, it's changing.'

Big James looked up and around. He shrugged. 'It could be, it changes fast, often does.'

He rubbed at his beard.

'I'm not going,' John said and James grimaced. He didn't appear to have a reply because he just stood there watching Simon and his brother moving away.

'Hey!'

A call rang out from behind. We all looked.

'Told you,' said James.

'I already knew,' said John. 'I told Simon.'

He looked fairly average. More slightly built than Simon or James, but bulkier than John, and dressed in the same kind of clothes. No great good looks or immediate charisma. Just a regular guy by the shore, waving to a couple of fishermen. He came closer and as he did two things happened. The heavens tore open and I recognised the young builder I had seen from the train window. A little older now, the face a little more weathered, the shoulders a little broader. Same smile though. I tried to recall if he'd been wearing jeans when I'd seen him previously, on that roof with his father, but for the life of me I couldn't. The Romans had certainly been recognisable with their stallions and armour and swaggering brutality. But I couldn't remember what the builders had been wearing. No matter, as Isabeth had said, this world seemed to be a mysterious montage of the Good Book melding with my own worldview.

A wind rocked in and threw the tranquil sea into chaos. Out on the water Simon and his brother wrestled with the sailing. The stranger walked up to James and said something I didn't catch. My ears and eyes were getting spattered with rain now. My clothes were sticking to me. The stranger didn't stop at James, he took a few more steps and the water must have been shallower than I thought because he kept going and his feet didn't disappear beneath the surface. He did stop eventually, waving to Simon. The big guy was drenched out there and his brother was quickly catching up too. They were starting to look worried, I guess even big fishermen have their limits. The water was more turbulent than ever, pushing the boat every which way. The stranger looked up and said something, then he repeated it a little louder. Some kind of order to someone or other. Fortunately then the wind began to drop and the rain took a break too. I looked at James and John, they were staring at the stranger. Beyond them I could make out some of the other fishermen. They were staring too. Something had happened here. Simon and his brother began rowing back to the shore, baling out water as they came. The stranger waited for them and took hold of the boat as it neared him. The weather was quiet again now and I did catch his next words to the brothers.

'Follow me,' he said.

I looked back, the train had gone. Along with my coffee. I was on my own again. I walked back towards the railway. The track had vanished. Not just the train and Al, but the whole line too. I was stumped for a moment so I looked to the water. Now the fishermen had vanished too. The boats were there, and the scene was poetically tranquil once again. But the men had gone, left their nets bundled up like discarded burger wrappers. It took me a moment to spot them again, they were disappearing up the nearby road, Simon up front with the stranger, John at the rear, the others in-between. I followed. I'm not sure why. I guess they seemed my only hope.

5. The Hillside

The wind blew up again, and I heard that sound of pages rustling on the breeze. I spun around on the spot, felt immediately dizzy doing it. I reached to steady myself and found my hand on a tree. I leant against it, then dropped and sat. The world span for a moment, as more rustling sounded. Then I heard someone clearing their throat. I looked up. It was the donkey. The talking, throat-clearing donkey.

'I have a big role coming up,' he said.

'What in *Shrek 5*?' I shot back.

He laughed. I know, it sounds ridiculous, but there was definitely laughter.

'Bigger than that,' he said. 'Gonna be a star.'

'Not yet you're not,' said another familiar voice.

It was the woman in white, she grabbed the animal and steered him away. 'Your time will come soon enough,' she said, and she gave his backside a gentle shove. He began to saunter away.

'I finished it,' he called as he went.

'Finished what?' I said.

'*Murder on the Orient Express*. I was right. I'd figured it out from page 10. I'm onto *Life of Pi* now. I can see the end already. I bet they all eat each other. I bet they do. And I bet they're not animals either. What they need on that lifeboat – is a talking donkey.'

He gave one last look back. 'That would spice things up a bit.'

'Go on, Shakespeare,' she told him.

He went back to his sauntering. Faded into the distance.

'Back in the action again then?' she said as she dropped down beside me.

'Yea,' I said, 'so soon too. I thought it looked so peaceful here.'

'Many people do. Nice biblical Galilee. Jesus walking around with his arms out and his halo on, making everyone happy.'

She shook her head.

'You mean… that guy… that was…'

'Really? Really? You saw all that and you didn't twig? Really?'

She clearly thought I was kidding, or mad, or just plain stupid. I didn't care.

'I'm just glad there are no smoking, building-eating, seven-headed dragons round here,' I quipped back.

Her rosy cheeks lit up with her smile and she flicked a few strands of hair away.

'Funny guy, eh?'

'No. I'm serious. Please tell me there are no killing machines here.'

She pursed her lips and thought for a moment. 'Well, there is the Roman Empire and that's pretty efficient – what you might call Crucifixions Incorporated. But there are no monsters. You'll be fine.'

'I'm not sure about that, I may still go nuts.'

She patted my leg, straightened and pulled me up. 'Come on, come see something good. Something that'll make you feel better.'

'Is it a long walk? Only I'm done walking.'

She turned me round to face the tree, but the tree was gone. There was instead a sweeping hillside, and the sudden sound of a thousand voices. Men, women, children, babies. The noise hit me like a speaker turned up to 11. I stepped back and crunched her foot.

'Ow!' she said and she pulled herself free.

She nursed her toes with one hand and pointed beyond the people with another.

'This lot,' she said, 'every one of them is here for him. Your friend by the water.'

There was a smudge in the distance, a stickman figure talking animatedly with the other smudges around him.

'They love him,' she said, 'he's brought them good news and they don't get much of that. Most of them see themselves as bits of scrap. He doesn't.'

'Yea, but they'll all turn on him, won't they? I know the story.'

'What d'you mean?'

'The crowds, they all crucify him.'

She gave me a strange look and blinked twice. 'Where'd'you get that from? It's not this lot that turn nasty. He's a people's champion. It's the people who have too much to lose. The authorities, the powerbrokers. They're the ones who organise their own rent-a-crowd to turn on him. Nothing to do with these folks. You should do your research.' She slapped me on the shoulder. 'Come on.'

She tugged at me again and we were suddenly over the other side of the crowd, a few steps from the stranger and his fishermen friends. She made me sit down again, turned and walked away. She was gone as soon as I could look for her.

'Here.'

It was the big fisherman, looking as gruff as ever. He held out his massive hand and it cupped a wedge of bread and some fish. I took it. It wasn't the way I'd cook fish but it was all right.

'Make the most of it,' he growled, 'there won't be plenty more where that came from.'

'Really?'

'No. Not if we're supposed to feed this shambles.' He waved a hand towards the crowd, showering crumbs as he did so. He moved on, reaching into a basket and pulling out another fistful. I watched him for a while then another voice brought me back to reality. Or rather, this unreal reality I was currently experiencing.

'Here.'

Another handful of bread and fish came my way. It was the young guy. John. He smiled.

'Oh no, it's okay,' I said. 'I already had some from the big guy, and I know you're short.'

'What d'you mean?'

'I know you haven't got enough for everyone.'

He threw back his head and laughed, a roaring, face-reddening laugh.

'You're joking. We'll never run out. Look.'

He showed me his basket, it was full to the brim.

'Started off with a child's supply of lunch, ended up with this banquet,' he said. 'And you know the best bit?' He indicated the crowd, and managed to do it without showering crumbs. 'This lot would never normally get to eat together. Not allowed to, see. Rich and poor, priests and prostitutes, sinners and saints. They're segregated. They don't allow it normally. But he's pulled a fast one, suddenly turned it into a picnic. Brought everyone together. Anyone's welcome. Here. You can have thirds as well if you hang around long enough.'

He shoved his food at me and I could do nothing else but take it.

I heard a grunt and a sigh and I swear the ground shook a little as the big fisherman dropped beside me. He smelt of fish and sweat, he was that close I got it immediately. He was staring at his open hands. There was more fish and bread in there.

'Look,' I said, 'it's really generous of you guys but I can't eat anymore…'

'How does he do it?' he said. 'How's he make it happen? How? How?'

He raised his gaze from his hands and stared at

me. His eyes were bloodshot and dark-ringed. He was not having the best of days.

'You should eat some of it, you look hungry,' I said, clutching at straws.

'I've no appetite,' he said, 'I work all hours of the night for this stuff.'

He held up a fish tail, it wilted quickly in his fingers.

'He just makes it happen, just like that.' He looked off into the distance. 'It's the wedding all over again.'

'Cana?' I said, as a bell rang in my head.

He nodded and looked back at me. 'You were there too then? I don't recognise you, but no matter. You heard? Six jars of water into wine. Like that.' He snapped those colossal fingers of his and the fish tail flew from his hand and landed on the arm of a boy a couple of feet away. I reached over and brushed it off, the boy stared at me and scowled.

'And you know what?' the big guy went on, 'he hardly drank any of it himself. Made it for everyone else. And, made it so the groom wouldn't look a total jerk. D'you think he's the deal?'

'The deal?'

'Yea. The Messiah. The one. You see, he isn't the way I was told. He doesn't hatch plans or give rousing speeches or curry favour with the right sort of people. If you were going to plot a revolution you'd do all that wouldn't you? He just does things like this. Make fish and bread. You know, when he met me he gave me a massive catch of fish. Free. Any other rabbi would have kept it for himself. But not him. He says it's so we don't have to worry about fishing for a while, so we can do some learning.'

He shook his head and stood up, as he moved I was hit by another wave of sweat and fish.

'I never wanted to be a disciple. Look at me. I know nothing about the prophets and the sages, and the law and interpretation. Seriously. My family are still laughing about this. I'm built for throwing nets in water and pulling out fish. That's what I do. And then one day he pitches up and gives me free fish and says I'll show you about catching other kinds of fish, and look at me. Stuck on a hillside giving away free bread.'

'Didn't Moses give people Manna?' I said in an inspired moment.

He sighed and threw me a sneer. 'Don't you start. I've already heard the murmurs. They all think he's the new Moses. Miracle bread. What can you do?' He was still muttering as he walked away.

'D'you want thirds?'

It was John, he was back with his grin. 'Told you, eh? Look at this.' He tilted his basket towards me, it looked fuller than when I'd last seen him. 'That's leftovers, I've been collecting them up.' He dropped down beside me. More sweat and fish.

'D'you know what I heard once?' he said, leaning in and giving me the benefit of his breath. 'When I was growing up, they told me about this old prophet called Ezekiel. You ever heard of him?'

'I've met him.' I couldn't resist it, I knew it would mess with his head but I was tired of covering up.

He gave me a strange look. 'I'm not talking about the man who fixes shoes. I know you know him, we all know him. Sometimes I wish I didn't. I'm meaning the prophet in the writings. He once said that God would feed his sheep. Right? God himself. Like a good shepherd. Don't you think that's weird? Jesus comes along and what's he doing?'

I didn't have time to reply before he went on.

'Feeding everyone. And calling himself a good shepherd. Spooky or what?'

I never got to tell him. He leapt up and started off, but not before he glanced back and gave me one last strange look. 'Oh by the way,' he called, 'somebody wants you. Over there.'

He snapped his fingers and pointed over the hill. I clambered up and followed his direction.

She was back. With her black hair and rosy cheeks. We stood together for a moment watching the throng on the hill stuffing down food, her arm round my shoulder. Then she turned me again and there it was. The railway line, sitting in the middle of nowhere. Totally out of time and in the wrong place. The rails rumbled and the train pitched up with its smoke and steam.

'There you go. You can enjoy your coffee now,' she

said.

Coffee? Had I told her about that?

I climbed on board and flopped down in the carriage. Al was in there, leaning back in the seat and twiddling with the radio. I'd only just got in when the door slid open again and Isabeth appeared with the coffee.

'Is it still hot?' I said.

'Course it is,' she said, 'I've only been gone a minute or two.'

6. The Resistance

The coffee was strong and tasted bitter. I did my best to hide the scowl. I failed.

'What's wrong?' she said. 'Coffee no good?'

I shook my head. The coffee was fine. At least everybody else seemed to think so. It was just me. I was the one who always found coffee too bitter and tea too bland. Nothing would hit the spot. Nothing fitted. I realised now that I'd felt that all my life. Things were either too bitter or too bland. Nothing fitted. That was probably another reason for my going to the bridge that night. Never mind. This train ride wasn't like that, no one could say it was bland or bitter. It was unpredictable, extraordinarily unpredictable, and every station ambushed me.

The carriage lurched and I spilt the drink. I couldn't help thinking that if Isabeth was still holding it she wouldn't have. I gave her a quick sideways glance. Yep. She was watching. She pulled a spotless handkerchief from her suit pocket.

'This help?' she said.

I took it and dabbed at the stain on my trousers.

'Any news of the sandwich maker?' I said, mostly to change the subject. 'And are we getting anywhere here? I mean are we any nearer to this great dream of breaking into paradise?'

Aladdin laughed. 'I'm having a good time,' he said.

'Al, you haven't been off this train yet,' I said.

'How d'you know? Maybe I get off after you do and get back on just before you come back.'

'Do you?'

He shrugged. 'Maybe.'

'Next time come with me,' I said. 'I'm throwing down the gauntlet. Next stop, we both go.'

Al looked back at me and his smile faded, then he looked at Isabeth. It might have been my imagination but I'm sure she gave the briefest of nods.

'Why d'you look at her?' I asked.

'Because it's not his adventure,' Isabeth said, and she blinked as she said it, precisely and only once.

'Not his adventure?'

She shook her head. 'No.'

I didn't get it. I looked back at Al. He shrugged and made hasty attempts to clean the smears and grit off his face, all that detritus he'd caught from sticking his head out of the window so much.

'Your coffee's getting cold,' Isabeth said.

I drank it down. It tasted strange after the bread and fish, like I was drinking something in the region of hot mackerel juice.

I pulled out my moleskine notebook and scribbled for a while. No one said anything more. Al retuned the radio. Another song came on – U2 singing about climbing high mountains and running and crawling and scaling city walls but still not finding what they were looking for. I knew what they meant. The train pulled up with another lurch and my pen scrawled across the page of my book.

'Come on then,' said Al. 'Let's go climb some highest mountains.'

Before I could stop him he was out of the carriage. I looked at Isabeth for help here and she just cocked her head towards the door.

'What about you?' I said.

She gave the smallest of headshakes. 'Someone needs to stay here and keep the seats warm.'

'I'll do it,' I said, 'I'll stay.'

Another tiny headshake. 'Not my adventure,' she said, and this time she said it with the faintest of smiles.

That annoyed me somehow. I got the feeling everyone knew way more than I did. I got up and left. Al was hanging about on the platform, kicking his feet against a nearby bench as he waited for me.

'There you are, dude!' he said hurrying over as I hovered in the doorway. 'Come on, let's do some exploring.'

He grabbed my shoulder as soon as I hit the platform and he tugged me towards the exit. I half expected to see the woman in white again, but the road outside was empty. Al pointed ahead.

'There you go – a mountain. Let's have that,' he said.

Aladdin saw life like that, something to be conquered, every mountain within his grasp. He rubbed his hands together. Keen for the challenge. As we went he kept whistling that song about not having found what he was looking for, so much so that it got into my head too and we were both stuck with it. Still, the weather was good and the trees and scenery around were buzzing with life. I wasn't sure where this road was taking us but I figured it couldn't be too bad. Certainly not to some seven-headed dragon's lair. I looked at Aladdin, he was walking with his usual casual swagger. At ease with the world. I wondered what he might be thinking. Then he let me know.

'D'you think I might have a chance with Isabeth?'

'Isabeth?'

'Yea, I know she's not my type but…'

'More like you're not her type.'

'Opposites attract.'

We walked on.

'Why did you look to her when I asked you to get off the train with me?'

'Err…' he was flummoxed there for a moment. For a long moment. I let the question hang in the air.

'So – what about it?' he said after a while, 'd'you think I have a chance?'

The road cut into the hills and that's when it happened. Suddenly we were surrounded and in trouble. Armed men, about our age, hands full of clubs and knives. Suddenly I was living my nightmare.

…lying by the road, off my head after another night out, as ever abandoned by my so-called friends, and yes, here we go

again, I grab at my pockets and discover the scabs have run off with my cash. My wallet's here but never more empty… the hand reaching for me doesn't go for my arm, it goes for my face instead. Slapping me hard, and again. A third time and I'm seeing stars. I feel a boot in my ribs and smell urine and mud on the leather. I tuck my head under my arms and hug the floor as the fists rain down on me. In my head I go somewhere else, a safe place, another world where these things don't happen. But the beating and the spitting and the cursing goes on…

'You're a long way from home,' one of the gang said, a tall thin guy, good-looking but for the pock marks on his face.

'Yea,' said the brutish guy next to him, his knuckles a mass of steel studs. 'You wanna watch yourselves.'

'Hey dudes,' said Al, 'let's all be cool. We're just going from A to B.'

'Well we own B,' said the tall guy, 'and we might own A as well.'

He lifted his club and let it fall back into his palm. it dropped with a resounding slap.

'Easy,' said Al. 'Who are you guys anyway?'

'Heroes,' said the brute with the knuckles, and a few of the others laughed. 'Yea,' he went on encouraged by the others, 'we're heroes, or we will be one day. When we've rid these parts of the Roman scum.'

'Yea,' said the tall guy, 'wanna join us?'

It was a test rather than an invitation. I could see

that. I'm not sure Al could though.

'We're busy,' was all he said.

'You know what they look like to me?' said the brute.

'No what?'

'They look like they're with that new guy. Jesus. Is that right? You with that Jesus gang?'

Al looked at me. I shook my head. If in doubt deny everything.

'No,' Al said.

It was true of course. We weren't with that group of disciples. We weren't with anybody except the sandwich maker, and we didn't even know where he was. That gave me an idea.

'You haven't seen a wild guy with red hair and rampant whiskers and odd shoes have you?' I cut in.

The tall guy raised his eyebrows. 'Oh, so the other one talks?'

'Well, that's who we're with,' I said. 'We need to find him. Maybe he's been this way.'

'Anyone going this way gets found by us. And dealt with.'

He lifted his club and let it drop again. The brute squeezed his knuckles and followed the sound of the club slap with the crack of his own bones. I looked around, suddenly the hills didn't look so green, the rocks were darker, a little more grim, there was a chill on the breeze. The chirp of birds and insects seemed to have died away.

'So you ain't with the Jesus gang? Are you with some other resistance fighters? There's plenty to go round.'

'He told you,' said Al, 'we're with the sandwich maker.'

'The what?' the gang laughed.

'The old crazy guy with the red tufty hair and the strange outfit. He's no harm to anyone. And neither are we.'

The brute leant towards the tall guy. 'I say we take them, they look to me like they're worth something. Maybe this sandwich man will pay good money.'

The tall guy left the circle and came closer. He walked round us, looking us up and down. He smelt of damp earth, like he'd spent a lot of time underground. At some point he'd certainly been through something with those pock marks.

'You can't be going somewhere through these hills,' he said.

'Can't we?'

'No. The only thing round here are the fighters. You either come here to hide, or you come here to fight. Which is it?'

The only plan I could come up with was the truth. 'We're lost.'

'You're lost?'

'Yea... we're looking around and we didn't know this was your territory.'

He screwed up his handsome features and gave an

ugly scowl. Which was no mean achievement considering his good looks. He made another lift and slap with the baseball bat.

'You seen this Jesus then? You didn't seem surprised when I mentioned him.'

'He has,' said Al, jabbing his thumb in my direction.

I nodded, wondering how he knew such things. I'd not had time to tell him much at all.

'They say he's powerful.' The tall guy kept walking round us, it was difficult to know where to look to make contact. In the end I stared at my leather baseball boots. They were looking well scuffed now.

'You don't have to worry,' I said.

The tall guy suddenly swiped in and jabbed his club under my chin, pushing my head back. 'Oh we're not worried,' he hissed, 'don't think we're worried.'

'I just meant he's no threat. He's not a resistance fighter.' It was a struggle getting the words out with that bat jabbing my throat, but I did my best.

'That's what you say. I heard he's planning something. Something at Passover. An uprising. They call him a rabbi but have you seen his followers, they're no religious types. Fishermen and rebels. He's a fighter all right.'

'Why not join him then?' I said.

He shoved the bat harder under my chin, then thought better of it and pulled it away.

'Yea,' said the brute, 'I've been saying that. Haven't

I? Two gangs better than one. He's got that zealot with him. What's his name? Simon, that's it. And also that Judas. We could easily get a message to them. I trust that Judas, he's a good guy.'

'Shut up,' said the tall guy, 'you don't know anything. Trust him do you? I reckon he'd sell his grandmother for a fist of fish. And then sell yours an' all.'

He turned his club towards the brute, waving it accusingly at the shorter guy. The brute cracked his knuckles in reply but his left eye started to twitch uncertainly and his gaze flitted about, looking to the others for support.

'Plus,' went on the tall guy, 'he fraternises with…' he spat, 'Roman lovers.'

'He what? What's fraternise?'

'He mixes with them, idiot, he helps 'em out. Those who love the enemy. Collaborators like Matthew and Zacchaeus both tax collectors. Both in bed with the…' he spat, 'Roman scum. Plus, there's a rumour he healed a Roman officer's orderly. What more d'you want? If he's the Messiah then he's here for us. Not the bleedin' crucifiers. Not the murdering pagans.' He spat again. And then again, a darker, thicker streak, as if to underline the first spit. The road fell silent. Somewhere a wolf howled. I glanced at Al, he was flicking his eyes back up the road, the way we had come. It was a mad idea but I think he was contemplating making a run for it.

'Barn's heard him. He's been to see him, he told me'

the brute blurted out.

The tall guy spun round and closed in on a muscly guy who was nervously brandishing a knife. Picking at the blade with his thumb nail.

'When? When did you go and see him?'

'It was a mistake, I swear. I didn't mean to, I was just passing by and I got drawn in.'

'Drawn into what?'

'People were giving away free food. I was hungry. That's all. There were thousands of them, and they all had free bread and fish. Good stuff too. What's wrong with that? We don't always get much here do we?'

The tall guy chewed on his lip as he kept coming closer. 'And you saw him?'

'Yea, kind of.'

'D'you speak to him?'

The tall guy had come very close now. The muscly guy swallowed and his prominent Adam's apple bobbed like a cork in rough water.

'Yea, kind of,' he said.

'What d'you mean – kind of?'

'I asked him a question. About my brother.'

'What about your brother?'

'He's rich, he got it from the family, I want half the money. It's only fair and it… well, it would help us wouldn't it?'

'And what did this Jesus say? Yes or no?'

The muscly guy frowned. 'Neither. He told a story,

about this guy who gets blessed with lots of crops and stuffs it all away in barns.'

'And?'

'And he died. God took his life.'

The tall guy scratched his head, just behind his left ear.

'He died? Was that some kind of coded message about killing Romans?'

'No. Don't think so. I think he was trying to say something about the destructive nature of being greedy.'

'The destructive nature of...?' The tall guy shook his head, he wasn't so sure. He studied the club in his hands, twisted it and then lifted it slowly and rested it on his shoulder. He didn't look happy. Not at all.

'Hey, Michael,' the brute suddenly called out.

'What?' the tall guy asked, looking deep into the muscly guy's soul and flexing his fingers on the club handle to get a better grip.

'They've gone.'

He swung round. It was true, we were half way back up the road. I'd taken Al's advice and legged it with him.

7. The Mountain

We were practically running. Al looked back at me (he had always been fitter) and grinned.

'That was a laugh, eh?' he said.

I thought I'd misheard him. A laugh? We nearly got beaten to a pulp. I looked back. The gang were little more than a blur of matchstick men now, in fact they were fading faster than I would have expected. I looked around, the scenery was flying by, almost as if we were sitting on the train again.

Smack! I ran straight into Al. He'd stopped to catch his breath. My eyes watered from the impact of the back of his head on my nose. I waited for my vision to settle down.

'Look!' he said.

He was pointing upwards, We were on the side of another mountain. There was a sudden white explosion at the top, like a camera flash. Something was glowing up there. Two or three figures were moving about. I didn't know whether to be worried or not. They didn't look like another gang of rebels, but what did I know? Al started on up.

'You sure that's a good idea?' I said.

He grinned at me. 'Of course it's a good idea. We have to try anything.'

I followed him at a distance. By the time we had reached the top there was just one man sat on a rock staring into space. The big fisherman.

'Simon?' I said, and he broke out of his reverie and looked round.

Al was impressed. 'You know this dude?' he said to me.

'Not really,' the smell of sweat and fish came back to me. 'I met him once.'

Simon stood up and looked us up and down.

'Do I know you?' he said. Then he snapped his fingers at me. 'You. You were at that wedding with all the wine.'

'No. I was on the hill with all the fish. You told me about the wedding when we were chatting.'

'Oh yea. Well you missed another one here.'

'Another what?' said Al.

Simon looked at Aladdin for a while, studied his inky jeans and his *Jaws* t-shirt.

'Big fish you got there,' Simon said.

Al looked down at his empty hands. Then he spotted the image on his chest.

'Oh right. Yea. It's a shark.'

Simon grimaced and shrugged. 'That would make some money. Catching one of those.'

'Might kill you,' Al told him with a big grin.

'I thought you didn't need money,' I said, 'You told me Jesus had given you a load of free fish.'

'He has,' said Simon, 'another miracle. Look, what are you two doing up here?'

'We saw the flash,' I said, 'we came to see.'

Simon turned and looked at a spot nearby. He

pointed.

'Right there,' he said and snapped his fingers. 'Just like that. Changed in an instant. Whiter than white. Like an angel or a vision or something.' He rubbed his beard. 'No not an angel. He was still a man you know. He was real. Too real. All this light was pouring out of him. And I swear Moses was right next to him. Standing here, smack in the middle of the promised land after all this time,' he said and he sat down again, shaking his head. 'Can't make it out. Can't make it out.'

'Shame we missed it,' said Al, walking over and crouching next to him. He looked over at me and winced and crinkled his nose.

'You were supposed to,' Simon said, 'it was just for us. He said that. Took us up here and left everyone else behind this morning. I can't help wondering…'

'Wondering what?' Al said, standing and dusting the grit off his knees.

'I'm not supposed to say really, he said talking about it could get him in trouble. Let's just say I recognised him the other day, saw him for who he might really be. Maybe that's why he brought us up here and showed us this. Bit like Elijah in the temple – seeing a vision.' He pointed to the spot again, rubbed his beard and nodded to himself. Then he looked over at us. 'But keep that to yourselves, right?'

Al leant forward and patted his shoulder. 'No bother mate, we can do that. But what about us, can we meet him?'

Simon stood up and dusted his hands off.

'Why not? Come down with me now.'

And he was off. It was all we could do to keep up as he took the path with his giant strides. As we neared the bottom we started to hear voices. There was a restless group of people waiting down there. Thankfully without any knives or clubs. The figure in the middle had his arm around the shoulder of a boy. Another man stepped up and hugged the child. Simon's brother came over, his face red as ever and his eyes wide.

'You missed another one!' he said, ignoring us. 'Boy just got healed. We tried to do it while you lot were away but we messed it up. His dad was well miffed. But it's all right. Jesus fixed it.'

And as he said this the figure in the middle of the crowd turned and looked at us. Might have been my imagination but I'm sure he looked right at me.

'Can we meet him?' Al asked.

'I said I'd bring them,' said Simon. 'You take 'em Andrew, you seem to be good at that kind of thing.' Simon's brother grabbed my shoulder and pulled us towards the crowd. They didn't part to let us through so he had to make a way by gouging a path between the bodies with his waving arms. Andrew burst through the final layer of people and there he was, that same guy, nothing special, just a regular corner of the street sort of bloke. But these people loved him. He looked tired. Al held out his hand and went straight up.

'I'm Aladdin Strike,' he said, 'I've heard a lot about you.'

The man raised an eyebrow. 'You know, I think I've heard a lot about you too,' he said.

That threw Aladdin for a moment. But only for a moment, he turned, pulled me over and introduced me. I panicked, and did what I always do when my head empties. I talked about anything.

'I heard about that wedding,' I said, 'well done. Good job. Sounded, you know, like er... like that's what you did – a good job. And... and with those fish too. Another good job. Up on that hill, you know.'

'Yea, I know,' he said, 'it's okay, you can calm down.'

'We've been looking for you,' said Al.

'Well you've found me all right,' he said.

We ran out of words after that, and Jesus' face looked suddenly drawn.

'It's not easy,' he said, 'all these people. Expectations. They want something I can't give.'

We looked round at the crowd. They were starting to drift away, wandering off in small clumps of friends and families.

'You can do anything,' said Al.

'No. Not really. They want me to fix everything now. Make everything all right. I can't do that. I'm here to do something else.' He looked back at us, stress crossing his face. 'What about you? Do you want something I can't give?'

Eager to please we both shook our heads with an enthusiastic, 'Oh no.' Al adding, 'Not at all.'

I didn't know what to say after that. The silence turned awkward. Andrew spoke up.

'Tell them one of your stories,' he said.

Jesus looked at us. Then he switched his attention onto me.

'Okay,' he said, 'what do you make of this? There was a man travelling once, and he found himself alone among bandits who beat him and took what he had. And as he lay there people passed by, and for various reasons they didn't help him. Then a stranger arrived and rescued him.' He put a hand on my shoulder. 'It wasn't a dream was it?' he said to me. 'You should find that stranger. Thank him.'

I shuddered. I didn't want to do that. I didn't need to revisit that night, it kept revisiting me too much.

'Find him, it'll set you free,' he said.

There was another awkward silence. Awkward for me anyway.

Then a small child ran up and grabbed his hand and his attention was torn from us. In a matter of seconds he was gone, dragged off into another conversation.

'What did he mean?' Al asked.

I was trying to formulate an answer when he spoke again.

'Never mind. Come on let's get back to the train.

I'm starving.'

Even as he said this the smell of smoke filled my nostrils and the train pulled in from nowhere. No one else seemed to notice but Al pulled me towards the line, opened the carriage door and bundled me on board. Neither of us noticed the shadowy images of the distant stickmen, watching us and making plans.

8. The Abduction

'I'm famished,' Al said as we burst in on Isabeth.

She had obviously been dozing as she took a moment to open one eye. Her silver glasses lay beside her on the seat and her eyes looked smaller without them.

'I'm not,' she said softly, closing her eye again.

'Well I am, I'm going in search of something edible,' and he abandoned us and forged his way down the corridor.

'Will he find some food?' I asked her, taking a seat opposite.

'You can find anything on this train,' she said, her eyes still shut.

A thought raced through my head so fast I barely had time to grab it and pull it back.

'Then in that case... I can find *him*.'

'Aladdin?'

'No.' I paused. 'You know who I mean.'

She smiled, her eyes still shut.

'Well, find him and you'll probably find food as well.'

I didn't care about food, I'd had seconds of bread and fish on a hillside. I got up and made my way along the carriage, looking in each compartment as I passed it. The train was still sparsely populated so I figured I wouldn't miss him when I found him. I left that carriage and crossed into the next. Barely anyone in that one, so I went on. Two more carriages and I couldn't even find Al. Only one carriage left. I checked each compartment with the expectation he'd be in there. I was nearly at the end when the train ground to a squealing halt. I heard footsteps behind me and turned to see Al running with a thick sandwich in his hand. Doorstop bread stuffed with green leaves, red tomatoes, grey meat and white sauce.

'There's something on the track!' he yelled, pushing open a door and leaping out of the carriage. We were beside a grass bank so I jumped out and followed him.

'Look!' He was standing there waving his sandwich at a huge tree trunk. It was lying across the rails looking like the fuselage of a crashed plane.

'Who put that there?' I said.

'They did,' Al said and he turned and pointed.

They quickly surrounded us. Again. That gang with the knives and clubs and bad attitude. The resistance fighters who thought very little about killing folks like us.

'You ran away,' said the tall guy with the pock-marked faced. 'We didn't like that.'

'Well you know how it is,' Al tossed back breezily.

'No. You tell us.'

The brute was standing beside the tall guy. He cracked his metal-encased knuckles.

'We had things to do. People to find.'

The tall guy swung his club onto the ground and leant on it like he was an old man with a walking stick.

'You talking about this "sandwich maker"?' he asked.

'Absolutely!' Al said.

'Good,' sparked the tall guy, 'Cause we wanna know about this sandwich maker you're following. Is he a rabbi? Or some new resistance leader. We asked around. No one's heard of him.'

'Well they should have – 'cause he's got special powers,' retorted Al with a gleam in his eye.

I looked around for the hole that might swallow me up. It wasn't there. I glared at Al.

'What are you doing?' I hissed, barely keeping my voice down.

'Telling him about the sandwich maker,' he said, all innocent.

'What do you mean? Special powers?' growled the brute. 'Like that Jesus of Nazareth? Miracle worker, is he?'

Al considered this. 'Not really. But he has worked one miracle I suppose.'

'What's that?'

I looked again for that hole – how was he gonna get out of this one? Al jabbed his finger at the train.

'Never seen one of those before have you?' he said.

The tall guy narrowed his eyes and looked past us to the steam engine. It was as if he'd not even noticed it till now.

'What is that?' he drawled. 'Some pagan machine? Some,' he spat into the dirt right by my foot, 'Roman invention?'

Al laughed. I wished he wouldn't do things like that. Just because we'd got away alive once didn't mean we would make a habit of it.

'No. It's a train. Way beyond your time.'

The tall guy shrugged.

'Any Romans on board?' he said, and he lifted the club and let it drop into his other hand with that familiar resounding slap.

'Doubt it,' said Al. 'But the sandwich maker is.'

'Why d'you tell them that?' I hissed, and the brute laughed at me.

'We got 'em worried,' he said.

'This looks like a Roman invention to me,' said the tall guy, waving his club at the train, 'your sandwich man working with the Romans is he? An Emperor lover is he? Like Herod and the Sadducees?'

I glanced back at the train. There were a few worried faces pressing against the carriage windows. Like street urchins peering at the privileged. No sign of the sandwich maker as far as I could tell though.

'He's self-employed as far as I know,' Al was saying, which of course meant nothing to them. I figured he'd be telling them about Tax Returns before long.

'Enough of this,' the brute said, and he stepped

forward and shoved Al out of the way. He fell against me and we both went sprawling. The tall guy led the gang towards to the train. The faces at the window instantly vanished. The rebels formed a line parallel with the carriage.

'On my signal – in,' said the tall guy and a dozen hands reached for the doors.

'No need for that, gentlemen.'

I'd only met him on that one occasion but I recognised his voice. He was leaning out of the window by Isabeth's compartment. The sandwich maker. His hair just as tufty as it had been before. His forehead still with that deep frown line, though his face now held a smile. I was beginning to wonder whether we'd ever meet again. But here he was. Red hair and thick antenna glasses. Flesh and blood and white coat.

9. The Parade

As he stepped down from the train I could see one of his pockets was stuffed with the wires we'd used to break in. The other held a bottle of the green liquid. He passed close by me as they took him away and there was a smell about him that I'd encountered before. It set my mind racing.

'What shall we do with these two?' Barn, the muscly one, asked, his Adam's apple bobbing violently as he lunged and grabbed at my arm. His grip was like a bench vice.

'Let's kill them now,' said the brute.

The tall guy took another look at us.

'Leave them for now,' he said, 'we can always pick them up later.'

They herded around the sandwich maker like farmers at a sheep market, shoving and pushing him as they made him start moving. One or two of them slapped his head and laughed. He looked immediately smaller and frailer amongst those thugs. It sickened me. This couldn't be right. What were they doing? And why weren't we doing anything?

Al started towards them but the brute turned on him.

'Come on there,' he taunted, 'let's see ya.' And he held up his bulky fists in a fighting pose.

Al glanced at me. I felt a coward but I felt afraid too. I did nothing. Apart from just standing there watching. Al shrugged and gave an apologetic smile. The brute sniggered and turned away. Eventually, when they were out of earshot, I said in a small voice, 'We have to do something.'

Al nodded, I knew he'd be up for action. 'Let's follow them, but keep your head down.'

The train had been stopped in the desert, but the road we took led us out from the wilderness to four hills and a city. We followed the jostling gang all the way there. As we neared the city the hillsides were filling up with tents and visitors. This was not going to be a quiet weekend.

'Passover,' Al said, 'Isabeth told me about it.'

'So why bring him here now?' I said.

'Apparently it's a good time for a revolution. The place'll be stuffed full with rebels and insurgents. Perfect for overthrowing the Romans.'

A sudden swell of sound shut him up. A group of men were coming towards us. I recognised Simon and his brother. James and John were there too. Then I spotted the animal.

'That's what he meant,' I said.

'Who?'

'The donkey. He told me he had a big role coming up.'

'The donkey told you that? How? Semaphore? Emoji?'

Okay, time to lay it on the line. He was after all just

as embroiled in this odyssey as I was.

'No, he can talk.'

'What??' Even Al was thrown by this. So much so that he roared with laughter.

'Listen,' I said, as Simon and the others came close. I looked right at the animal. 'Your big day then?' I said.

It didn't bat an eyelid. No clearing of the throat, no braying and, most obviously, no small talk. The group just went on by and he went with them. Simon didn't bother acknowledging me but his brother spotted me, nodded and threw us a smile. Still nothing from the donkey though.

'How's *The Life of Pi*?' I called out. 'Were you right about the end?'

Nothing. No quips, no back chat, no pithy remarks.

'A talking donkey eh?' Al said when they'd gone and we were staring at their backsides.

'He can talk, he can talk!' I insisted, but Al rolled his eyes.

'Yea, don't tell me, he can fly as well. And make a full English breakfast.'

I didn't bother arguing. There was nothing to prove really. I knew what I knew. And I'd make sure that donkey knew too when I caught him alone next time. We went on in silence. I looked for the sandwich maker but the gang of rebels had melted into the throng of people. We'd lost them. So I kept an eye on the donkey instead and we followed Simon and his mates. Maybe they would lead us to the others. A vain hope but I clung to it.

As we drew near the city John took hold of the donkey and one of the group climbed on. What was this all about? Simon and James started bellowing at people to make a way and then everyone started noticing. A chant started up about a new king, and others caught on. It was quiet at first but then the noise soon rippled through the crowd. The nearer we got to the city the louder the chanting became. In the end there were people jamming the streets, waving branches and throwing their coats to line the way. I spotted a few weapons too. More than a few. The longer this went on the more weapons I spotted. Knives, swords, clubs, bits of wood. Nothing too prominent, most held below waist level, or being passed from man to man. Clearly, in some people's minds, this wasn't just a peace parade. I looked for the rebels again, but there was no sign of them. There were soldiers though. Gleaming Romans looking none too pleased. They were all eyeballing the man on the donkey, every last one of them ready for trouble. The procession kept moving and the crowd grew louder. The soldiers flexed their fingers and made moves towards their weapons. All it needed was someone to shout 'riot' and there'd be all hell breaking loose here. I mentioned as much to Al but he didn't seem worried.

'We need to track down the sandwich maker,' he

said. 'Do a bit of rescuing. A bit of saving the day.'

I wasn't so sure, it was a nice idea, but amongst all these people? There was surely no chance of sighting them...

'There,' said Al, and he pointed.

He was right. A little further along the road, waiting by the side, in a break in the crowd. They were waiting for the procession to roll up. Al grabbed me and shoved me through the crowd, somehow he got us within a few steps of the rebels. The sandwich maker was being held by the brute and the muscly guy, Barn. He didn't look too bad, a little older maybe with a few bruises perhaps, but he didn't look scared. Then the man on the donkey came by, and the gang turned their attention to him. The tall guy went straight up and grabbed the animal to stop it. There was a hurried conversation with the man riding it. The tall guy stepped back looking taken aback. The muscly guy let go of the sandwich maker and went over to the man on the donkey. He didn't look taken aback at all and had a few words with the man. Then Simon and James came through and they pushed the tall guy away. He didn't like that and neither did the brute. They exchanged a few insults. It looked like a fight was brewing. Then the man on the donkey called out and James and Simon hesitated and pulled back. The rebels let them go and the parade moved on. The tall guy still looked a little stunned. He stood watching as the people moved on. Eventually the brute shouted at him and he broke out of his stupor. He turned and looked back at his men.

'Come on,' I heard him say, and they moved off.

Now we had sight of them we kept close. They slipped out of the city and took a road into one of the hills. So we did too. As we went I took a last look back at the city streets. The crowds were dispersing, there seemed to be a kind of disappointed murmuring in the air. The man on the donkey was walking away from the crowds. The whole thing seemed to have fizzled out. No uprising on the agenda.

10. The Dream

We lost them. No idea how, one minute we were right on their tail, the gang snaking in a single line with the sandwich maker slap in the middle, the next we rounded a bend in the hill and they'd gone. Taken some secret path known best to bandits and fugitives. We doubled back to see if we'd missed something, and before we knew it a wind whipped up, throwing us back against the raised ground. There was that sound again, the rustling pages. The images span and blurred and suddenly clouds of smoke and steam engulfed us. When they cleared we were on level ground away from the hills and the city. And there was the railway line again and the train sitting waiting for us. This time though Isabeth was there at the door, pushing it open and leaning out to call us in. We went.

'Did you find him?' she asked, looking a little flustered. A totally new look for her.

Al shook his head. 'Lost him,' he said. 'But there's something going down in the city.'

'I know,' she said as she ushered us back into the carriage. There was hot food on a tray on one of the seats. Meat, bread, rice and vegetables.

'What do you mean – you know? How d'you know?'

She shot a look at Al. Al said nothing, he just kept eating. She handed me a plate and I kept picking at the food.

'There's more going on here than you know,' she said, straightening her glasses.

'Clearly,' I said. 'Am I the only one who doesn't get it?'

She sat down opposite me, looked me straight in the eyes and spoke carefully.

'The sandwich maker set all this up,' she said.

'I know, he worked out a way to break into the Bible and now we're all stuck in a train trying to find him so we can get out again.'

She shook her head. 'We're not stuck. This is as it should be. This is all part of your adventure.'

'My adventure? What d'you mean?'

She cleared her throat and adjusted her position slightly, Al went to the window to stick his head out but she called him back and pointed to the seat beside her. He rolled his eyes, puffed out his cheeks and sat.

'Tell us about your dream,' she said. 'That recurring nightmare.'

'How d'you know about that? How does everyone know about that? Jesus knew about it an' all. I don't get this.'

'Go on,' said Al, spooning some food into his mouth, 'tell us about it.'

I looked at them, and shuddered inside. Then I shut my eyes and, against my better judgement, started talking.

'It was a while ago now. Maybe a year, actually no,

a little more. I was working in a factory back then, filling in time,' I sighed, steeled myself and started reliving the thing. Again. 'I'm lying by the road, off my head after another night out, as ever abandoned by my so-called friends, and yes, here we go again, I grab at my pockets and discover the scabs have run off with my cash. My wallet's here but totally empty. They'll laugh about it tomorrow as we shift stuff in the factory, and I'll put on a brave face and join in, but it's no joke to me. Happens too often. Me left nursing the same old headache and short of cash to see me through the week yet again. I hear a step and think that for once one of them has come back for me, maybe to help me up, maybe to apologise, maybe to give me at least my bus fare home. But the hand reaching for me doesn't go for me arm, it goes for my face instead. Slapping me hard, a couple of times.

'After the third strike I'm seeing stars. I feel a boot in my ribs and smell urine and mud on the leather. I tuck my head under my arms and press into the floor as the fists rain down on me. In my head I go somewhere else, a safe place, another world where these things don't happen. But the beating and the spitting and the cursing goes on.
On.
And on.
And on.
May well only be a matter of moments, but it feels like forever.

'Eventually, after ripping off my jacket and tearing open my pockets – I think there may be a knife involved – they saunter away into the darkness with my watch, phone and empty wallet. And I never once got a look at their faces. I have no idea how many there were. I'm just left with my pain and bruises and broken spirit. Verminous scum.

'It takes me a long time to summon the strength and the courage to look up, just in case one of them is waiting there to catch me full in the face. But eventually I chance it. There is silence. No one there. Then I see the lights of a car. It doesn't slow. Just flies by, either not seeing me bundled there on the pavement, or not caring. Another car. It slows a little, then speeds up again. They're probably worried that I could be a trap. I could be perfectly healthy there, just lying as bait for the first wealthy nightclubber stupid enough to stop and get out and get mugged by the waiting gang. Well, the waiting gang has long gone. Thank God. It's just me, waiting for a hand up. Three more cars, one slowing for a moment while the others just fly by. Then the sound of heels. Clack, clack, clack. Stilettos and probably three or four in the group. I can hear talking. They slow down. Stop. Make cautious whispers to one another. They cross the road, walk by on the other side. Who can blame them? Why wouldn't they? They're vulnerable on a night like this. The heels clack away and fade. Clack,

clack, clack. A long time goes by with nothing. I force myself to sit up and lean back against the wall. I feel blood on my chin and more on my cheek. One eye is cut and my mouth too. I wonder about my ribs, they took a pummelling. Every time I snatch at a breath there is pain down there.

'More footsteps. Heavier, male probably. A couple of guys bantering about football. They slow up, stop, two faces drop into my line of vision. I try and smile but breathe at the wrong time and end up scowling at them. They smile back. One of them has a gap-toothed grin. They both have shaved heads and pierced lips.

"Ouch, looking rough mate," one of them says.

I nod and grimace. They look at each other.

"Here," says the other, "I guess they took your stuff, so have this…"

'He hands me a couple of tenners and a rag which I have to assume is clean.

"Should get you a bus ride home and a burger. We got a party to crash. Cheers."

'And they go. I watch, pressing the rag to my eye. It stings. I get confused and press the tenners to my mouth. That does little good. More time passes. I'm getting cold. They took my jacket and I don't know where they threw it. The pain in my ribs is getting worse. As I start to shiver it's a nightmare. More time goes. I start to fade into some other reality. I don't hear the steps, just feel a hand shaking me. I look up.

'An old guy frowns then smiles at me. He pulls out a phone, presses buttons, sits on the kerb and waits with me. I come in and out of consciousness. He takes the rag and cleans my face up. Takes off his jacket and struggles to put it round me. He presses buttons on the phone again. There's some kind of hold-up with the ambulance. He hangs up and dials again. Makes some kind of deal for a car. We wait. A taxi pulls up. The driver is reluctant to take me. At some unknown point I have thrown up on myself and smell terrible. I hadn't noticed myself but it matters to him. The old guy is fierce with his persuasion. They bundle me in the back, next thing I know I'm in casualty, the old guy hurrying people along, getting up and talking then sitting down and doing his best to warm me up.

'Finally my name is called and they take me in. I have three broken ribs, a fractured arm and multiple bruises. I never see the old guy again. A few weeks later I get a parcel in the post. It contains my jacket – repaired and cleaned – along with my watch, my phone and my wallet. The wallet is stuffed with new notes, more money than I've ever had in there. There is no letter or return address.'

11. The Thunder

'It wasn't a dream was it? It really happened.' Isabeth said when I'd finished.

I nodded, said nothing.

'Why d'you never tell me about this before?' Al asked.

'Well... we don't do that, do we?'

'Do what?'

'Talk about this stuff.'

An awkward silence.

'You know who rescued you that night?' Isabeth asked after a while.

I grimaced and shook my head. 'Not a single idea.'

'Are you sure?'

'Of course, how could I know? I...' Then it came back to me. That familiar smell when he had walked past me.

'Wait a minute.' I thought about it again. 'Are you telling me... it was him – the sandwich maker?'

She nodded. Al looked at her then grinned at me.

'You betcha!' he said.

'But... how... I mean the guy who rescued me was older... I think.'

'Was he?' Isabeth asked.

I didn't know now. I'd just known he was older than me and didn't seem that young. Yet, thinking about it now, he had been capable of doing plenty. I didn't remember his hair being red and grey, but then, I didn't remember what colour it was, I hardly set eyes on him in my beaten state. Kept staring at the ground, or people's shoes as they passed by. It was just that smell I had registered, the same one I had caught when the gang walked him past me.

' So... what? He set all this up...' I looked around the carriage, pointed out of the window, 'for me?'

She nodded. They both nodded.

'He kept an eye on you after that night. He tracked down the jacket and the watch and the phone. He went to a lot of trouble.'

'For me? This is all for me? Why? A trick? A joke?'

'Absolutely not. Just the opposite. He did it because he's an extraordinarily compassionate man, and the more he saw the way you were going, the more troubled he was.'

'But come on! It's not like I'm a criminal or anything.'

'No, not yet. But you were in trouble. Drifting, damaged, wasting your life. Maybe he could see the future in a way that you couldn't.'

I sat there in silence. I felt, all of a sudden, cheated and angry, along with frustrated and bewildered. I felt like I'd been under surveillance.

'So this is what? A wake up call of some kind?' I said.

'Maybe. It's a way of showing you another reality.'

'How come you know all this?' I looked from Isabeth to Aladdin and back again. Aladdin was grinning at me and nodding a lot.

'He told us. We care. We really do.'

And at that moment the train pulled up again. I glanced out of the window, there was more cloud and steam than ever. The plumes were thick beyond the glass there. I left the carriage and went to look outside. A huge cloud had dropped over the train. In fact it was quickly disappearing as I watched, engulfed by the dense grey smog. Suddenly thunder cracked overhead and a moment later lightning carved a jagged fork through the smoke. A violent wind kicked up and began shoving me about. It was as if I was stuck to the hand of a giant and he was trying to shake me off. I battled for a while against the wind and forged through the thick smoke. Eventually the cloud thinned out and a mountain rose up in front of me. My feet were kicking through sand and there was a wall of heat waiting as I emerged from the smoke. The cloud rose and drifted towards the mountain. More lightning cut through it as it went. Thunder rumbled and the ground shook. I jumped as I heard scuffling either side of me and I looked left and right to see Isabeth and Al right there.

'Where are we?' I yelled against the sound of the thunder.

'Sinai,' said Isabeth. 'The place where God descended on the mountain.'

I turned and looked again. There was fire in the sky now and the sound of the thunder was growing.

'That's God?' I asked.

'A physical manifestation of his presence,' she said.

As her words died away so did the thunder. Bit by bit the clouds dissipated and a huge gleaming figure rose up from it. I squinted at the light pouring from the image, it was like a giant halo glowing around him and beneath his feet a pavement of brilliant sapphire began to appear. There was no sound now and yet it was as if the air was teeming with the most incredible music. The whole thing was a kaleidoscope of light and colour and splendour. A Technicolor, 3D experience that no big screen could replicate.

We watched in silence, even Al was speechless. Eventually, and I have no idea how long we stayed and looked on, the image faded away again and for a while there was nothing but an overwhelming sense of peace. Then that dissipated and we dropped to our knees and fell into the sand.

'That's God?' I asked again.

They both nodded. More silence.

'And yet,' Isabeth began, 'you held him in your arms.'

She looked at me, 'Extraordinary isn't it?'

'When? When did I hold him in my arms?'

She smiled. 'Don't you remember? You helped rescue him,' she said, 'from the dragon.'

And suddenly it all came back to me. Holding the crying child as his teenage mother climbed out of that tunnel.

'That was God?'

'Yes,' she said. 'The Christmas baby Jesus. Did you have no idea?'

I had not. Perhaps if I'd known I would have been a little more careful. And a lot more nervous. I might well have been in danger of dropping him. I could barely get my head around that. God in the guise of a baby, right there in my arms. He was so small, so vulnerable. How could that be? She saw me shaking my head.

'Can't work it out?' she said. 'Neither can I. But then… I'm not God.'

'What about the dragon? What was that?'

She thought for a moment. 'The enemy. The darkness. King Herod and a million other destructive tyrants. The devil in disguise.'

'It came so close,' I said.

'Yes. But you helped them get away.'

12. The Graveyard

The smoke fell suddenly again and it set us coughing and shielding our eyes. As it cleared we heard voices. Men were shouting and issuing commands. Harsh, brutal men issuing harsh, brutal commands. We were outside the city again, another crowd lined the way. Soldiers were pushing three men along the road. There was blood and whips, wooden beams and a beating drum. There was wailing too, women crying and calling from the crowd beside the road. We kept our heads down, followed and watched. They took the three men up a gaunt hill and set about fixing them to crosses. The sound was sickening as the nails skewered the bodies to the wood. I moved a little closer and narrowed my eyes to get a better view.

I recognised two of the men there. The young fisherman John, he was crouching in the dirt, his face contorted with grief. I spotted him first, no sign of any of the others though. And then I saw the man who had been on the donkey. The man who told me about my dream and told me to look for the sandwich maker. The baby I'd held in my arms. Jesus. No comfort for him now. The dragon had finally won. He was up there, suspended, pinned between the two others, no chance of escaping over the border now. Nailed up like a piece of raw meat, a discarded carcass casting a forlorn shadow over these murderous, desperate, hurting bloodlands. The pain, the gravity, the meaning of it all cut into me in a way I'd never felt before.

Then I spotted a third man I recognised. I couldn't believe it. It was the tall guy, the leader of the rebels. Somehow they'd got him too, taken his club and pinned him up there beside Jesus. He looked in a bad way but as we watched he seemed to turn to Jesus and say something. The man in the middle looked back at him and replied. I don't know why but I figured Jesus must have been saying something good to him. Suddenly everything went dark. The ground trembled and there was a low rumbling in the air. There was no smoke or fire, but it put me in mind of that mountain. The presence of God shaking everything. A lone cry went up from the crosses. The ground shook again. Isabeth pulled at my arm.

'We need to go,' she said.

'Why?'

'Because of the train.'

'We're leaving this, now? The crucifixion, this monumental moment, because *I have a train to catch*?'

'I'm afraid so.'

She pulled me away and Al followed. We said nothing as we walked with our heads bowed watching our steps as we put one foot in front of another. The journey may only have been a matter of minutes, but the weight of each step made it feel much longer. The gloom continued for a while when suddenly there was the sound of a splintering crack. I looked up. There was another crack, then another. It was painful on the ears. We were trekking through a graveyard and bits of the ground were opening up, like a meringue breaking when you cut into it. A hand emerged here and there, other limbs protruded from the broken rock. I thought of Ezekiel and his valley of bodies.

'What's going on?' I said.

'New life,' Isabeth said. 'Resurrection.'

Al just said, 'Cool.'

We went on, walking through the resurgent tombs as if there was nothing strange going on. Like commuters ignoring the drunks on the tube. I looked back as we left the graveyard and saw bodies climbing up and out. With the darkness till brooding overhead it was like something out of an old horror movie. But these folks didn't look like the undead. Wisps of smoke washed across our way and suddenly there it was again, pulling up like a ghost train outside the city of the recently dead. We got on.

'Is that it? Can we go home now?'

'Of course not. We came to break into paradise didn't we?' said Al.

'I thought we were looking for the sandwich maker,' said Isabeth. 'My uncle,' she added softly.

'Oh yea,' Al replied, his voice quiet too.

The darkness deepened outside as the train rattled on.

I was pretty exhausted and I think the others were too. When we all fell asleep I don't know, but I dreamt again.

There I was once more lying by the road, drunk and bewildered, grabbing at my pockets and discovering that I have no cash. My wallet's here but never more empty. They'll laugh about it tomorrow as we shift stuff in the factory, but it's no joke to me. Happens too often. Me left nursing the old headache and short of cash to see me through the week yet again. I hear a step and know that for once one of them has come back for me, maybe to help me up, maybe to apologise, maybe to give me at least my bus fare home. But the hand reaching for me doesn't go for my arm, it goes for my face instead. Slapping me hard, and again. A third time and I'm seeing stars. I feel a boot in my ribs and smell urine and mud on the leather. I tuck my head under my arms and press into the floor as the fists rain down on me. In my head I go somewhere else, a safe place, another world where these things don't happen. But the beating and the spitting and the cursing goes on.
On.
And on.
And on.
A few seconds feeling like forever.

Eventually, after ripping off my jacket and tearing open my pockets – I think there may be a knife involved – they saunter away into the darkness with my watch, phone and empty wallet. Cars fly by. Then the sound of heels. Clack,

clack, clack. I can hear talking. They slow down. Stop. Make cautious whispers to one another. They cross the road, walk by on the other side. Who can blame them? Why wouldn't they? They're vulnerable on a night like this. The heels clack away and fade. Clack, clack, clack. A long time goes by with nothing. I force myself to sit up and lean back against the wall. I feel blood on my chin and more on my cheek. One eye is cut and my mouth too. I wonder about my ribs, they took a pummelling. Every time I snatch at a breath there is pain down there. More footsteps. Heavier, male probably. A couple of guys bantering about football. They slow up, stop, two faces drop into my line of vision. I try and smile but breathe at the wrong time and end up scowling at them. They smile back. One of them has a gap-toothed grin. They both have shaved heads and pierced lips.

'Here,' says the generous one, 'Have this…'
He hands me a couple of tenners and a rag which I have to assume is clean.

'Should get you a bus ride home and a burger. We got a party to crash. Cheers.'

And they go. I watch, pressing the rag to my eye. It stings. I get confused and press the tenners to my mouth. That does little good. More time passes. I'm getting cold. They took my jacket and I don't know where they threw it. The pain in my ribs is getting worse. As I start to shiver it's a nightmare. More time goes. I start to fade into some other reality. I don't hear the steps, just feel a hand shaking me. I look up. And I can barely believe it. For the first time I see him, my vision no longer blurred, the pain in my head temporarily subsiding. It is him. The sandwich maker. Not so old after all. He frowns then smiles at me. He pulls out his phone, presses buttons, sits on the kerb and waits with me. I come in and out of consciousness. He takes the rag and cleans my face up. Takes off his jacket and struggles to put it round me. He does all that, cleans me up and calls an ambulance. When that fails he calls the taxi and uses his persuasive powers. Before I know it I'm in casualty, the sandwich maker hurrying people along, getting up and talking then sitting down and doing his best to warm me up. Finally my name is called and they take me in. I have three broken ribs, a fractured arm and multiple bruises.

I never see him again. At least not until that night. On that bridge. And suddenly, there I am, right back there. Mind awash with darkness. Looking down into the water below. Wondering how cold it is and knowing I'll soon find out. The life at the factory too much, the 'friends' there have worn me down with their jibes and tricks. Plus life's disappointments, and its lack of purpose and direction, now hang like dead weights around my neck. I've spent too long wearing the memories of that mugging, the lingering fears festering like scars that just will not heal. Inhibiting medallions I can't seem to shake off. Noisy, polluting traffic forever in the back of my mind. The nightmares colour everything now; the aftershocks linger, and occasionally resurface, like belated tremors of an earthquake that has weakened the foundations of my being.

The whole mess is one fatal concrete overcoat that will help me sink all the faster in that cold dark water. Sink and never come out again. I stand there for the longest time, staring into the bleakness of the abyss below. The seconds start to feel like hours and for a while I just stay there, appreciating the wondrous anonymity of hovering between life and death. No one cares, no one knows I'm here. I'm invisible. And now that life has no hold on me I feel a strange, heady kind of bliss. I guess this all sounds a bit melodramatic but it was how I felt back then. Things had been bad, my confidence had leaked away. And the treatment from my 'friends' at work had left me with no appetite for much of anything. Rekindled too many school day memories of bullying and isolation. So I've embraced the darkness and I've come to this, my way out. The notion has been hovering on the doorstep of my mind for a long time.

I steel myself and prepare for my last seconds on earth. Tick… tick…tick… 3…2…1… then I hear those footsteps, not far enough away, and I'm aware of someone approaching and stopping nearby. I wait but the figure doesn't go anywhere and I know I can't go through with it.. Not tonight anyway, so I make a back-up plan. I'll do it tomorrow. No problem, I'll finish it then. I walk away, chancing a glance back as I go. And I see him. It's the sandwich maker. In the shadows. I hadn't known it before, but now I do. The next morning I get a parcel in the post. It contains my jacket (repaired and cleaned), my watch, my phone and my wallet. The wallet is stuffed with notes, more money than I've ever had in there. There is no letter or return address. There is hope in the world after all. There is light. My resolve to end things weakens. I never go back to that bridge after all. So then I'm back in the sandwich maker's dimly lit back room, holding vials of green liquid and plugging the supple white cables into my flesh. The smell of bread and sandwich fillings permeates the place, so thick you can almost see it, like fog. Prawns. Bacon. Beef. Ham. Sausages. Salad. Mayo. Onions. Eggs. Sardines. And the aroma seems to act like smelling salts, bringing me round, stirring my senses.

13. The Glory

I woke in the depths of night to see Al curled up across three quarters of our seat and Isabeth slouching against the back rest of hers. It cheered me up a little to see her not quite so pristine perfect, her hair chaotic and her glasses slipping the merest fraction off her nose. I reached across and eased them off and onto the seat beside her. My mouth felt dry, I needed some kind of lubrication. I slipped out into the corridor. And that's when I saw what was happening outside. History was flashing past the train. Scenes I'd just lived through were replaying before my eyes. Ezekiel in his rainbow clothes, bringing those dusty bones back on their feet. Noah and his boat, and the bad guys with their slings and rocks. The loud-mouthed, ruddy-faced woman holding court under her palm tree; Joshua meeting that massive warrior; Isaiah in his coughing car; Abram and Melchizidek sharing their bread and wine. Then I saw Rizpah, still shooing the birds from her dead sons, and Ruth helping the bitter but beautiful Naomi. The donkey, the woman in white, Jeremiah down his well, they all kept coming. Like cartoon doodles in the corner of a notepad, the pages flipping fast and bringing them to life. Like pages tumbling from an ancient comic book, creased and worn from age, and spilling across the night.

Suddenly the radio kicked into life. It had been dead

up till now. I dived back into the carriage to grab it before it woke the others. It was The Eurythmics, Annie Lennox's soulful voice powering out and singing about saving the world today. I couldn't see any on/off switch so I pressed the transistor against my chest to muffle the noise and took it back out into the corridor. I went on watching the scenes unfolding to the radio soundtrack. Must have been a Eurythmics double because *The Miracle of Love* came on. It was the kind of miracle that would take away my pain, Annie was assuring me. It would come my way and make a difference, reaching all those hidden sorrows.

She sang on for a while then faded away and I heard the sound of rustling pages again just as the sun broke over the horizon. It raced across the sky and the moon followed it and died again. Another sunrise. Two days in the course of so many minutes. I was still clutching the radio and a hopeful sound seeped from it. I held it away from my chest a little, letting more music out. It fitted the breaking of the dawn perfectly. Coldplay's *Life in Technicolour*. As it played the sun rose at a more natural rate. I felt oddly hopeful. No idea why. I just stood there soaking up the glory of that morning. No more racing comic book pages. Just the gentle power of that new day out there. The warmth, the light, the colour. I heard the door open behind me. The music went on. I didn't need to turn, I caught the smell of her perfume.

'Beautiful isn't it?' she said, her voice croaking a little from sleeping.

She rubbed her eyes.

'Something's happened,' I said.

She glanced down at the radio. 'That's appropriate,' she said.

'Is it?'

'Yes. The third day. The *new* day. Resurrection moments. *Life in Technicolour*. He's back.'

'Who is?'

'The man on the cross. Jesus. You know all about that. Don't you?'

She looked carefully at me.

'Of course. Well, yea, I guess so.' I was trying to work out if this was some kind of trick question. 'I've known about it for a long time,' I said. 'Of course I have. But…'

'But what?'

'Well… *believing* it is another thing entirely isn't it?'

'Oh absolutely,' she said. 'Knowing and believing. Hearing and doing. They can be as far apart as two worlds. Two planets. Don't you think?'

I dropped the radio and it clattered on the floor, the battery compartment spilling open on impact. I reached down and picked it up, expecting to have to scrabble about for the batteries, but there were none. I looked inside. The compartment was empty.

'There are no batteries,' I said. 'Weird.'

She gave me a little smile. 'Anything's possible,' she

said.

I looked out of the window again. 'I saw an epic series of images while you were asleep,' I said. 'Places I've been to in the last couple of days. People I've met. Things I've done. All playing outside this window like scenes from a movie. What's it mean?'

'I think it means that... these nights and this morning... they're a kind of fulfilment.'

I decided I'd need to chew on that. I didn't tell her, but I think she knew anyway.

Just at that moment there was the far distant sound of grinding, like a stone moving from a tomb. At least I think that was the sound. It was so subtle that I'm not sure if she heard it or not. I looked out of the window and strained to hear it again. But there was nothing more.

'What about the sandwich maker?' I asked, after a while.

The train began to slow.

'Looks like we're about to find out,' Isabeth said.

Part Three
Paradise

270

1. Unfinished

Isabeth went back into the carriage and woke Al, then she scooped up a small canvass packet and slipped it into a pocket inside her grey jacket. Al clapped his hands as we climbed down from the train.

'Right,' he said, 'let's find some action.'

She frowned at him.

'Oh yea, and find your uncle of course,' he threw in quickly.

We had arrived at the cleanest, brightest station I had ever seen. No litter, no graffiti, no smells of oil or grease in the air. No fast fleeting, smut-covered mice racing across the tracks every now and then. Everything was clean and fresh. Even the smoke from the train had changed colour. It was now a heady mixture of silver and purple. The place was incredible. I couldn't make it out really. Isabeth waved us towards the exit and as we left the station we found ourselves on a broad sweep of road, a gleaming rainbow path leading towards the biggest gates I'd ever seen. Towering up ahead of us like a couple of gem-studded cliff faces. Narnian street lamps lined the way like benign sentries, there to warm your heart and encourage your steps. And between our feet, starting small, a thin strand of flowing water, a shimmering finger of stream running down the centre of the path. The constant ripples throwing out silver, dancing reflections across our hands and faces.

As we approached the gates they swung wide and we ventured in. With each footstep the leafy, vibrant world beyond revealed itself. Warmth, light, colour. Trees, plants, bushes. Not a dead or decaying thing in sight. Life in technicolour. Small creatures ran to look at us, birds flew in and crowded the branches of the trees. There wasn't a single lacklustre plant anywhere. All the fruit was fresh and ripe and ready for the picking. The trees were flooded with unusually shaped apples and pears and other succulent fruit. Nearby bushes gushed with berries of all shapes and sizes. There were plants I'd never seen before. And as for the combined aroma... well, I heard Al let out a whoop and a 'Wow!!!' and then another whoop and another 'Wow!!!' And then he did it again.

The whole thing crowded our senses. A kaleidoscope of scents and sights and smells. Indescribable. Filling the air and zapping the senses. It made you feel instantly welcome and at home. But more than that. Peaceful and invigorated. Tranquil and inspired. At ease in your own skin. I felt energy seeping into my exhausted bones. A million times better than that feeling you get in the early morning of a summer's dawn when the sun comes up and it's already promising to be a good, good day. There was music in the very atmosphere too, melody in the very air we were taking in. Any sense of reserve melted away. My defences fell and the feeling was a truly exhilarating one. We walked on, smoothing our fingers against the textures. Lapping up the luxury of this untainted life. I'm telling it to you now, reaching for phrases and descriptions, but of course no words could really take you there. What I'm telling you is nothing more than a pale shadow of a dim reflection of the wonder of it all. But it's something. And to tell you that this description is insufficient might well give you more idea of how incredible the experience was, rather than the description itself.

As we passed a particularly dazzling tree Isabeth reached for a branch and pulled free a couple of dynamic leaves. She took a tiny leather pouch from her pocket and stuffed them inside.

'There you go,' she said. 'A little keepsake.'

'Can you take that out of here?'

'Try and see,' was all she said.

I pocketed the leaves and we went on. We followed a glistening river, the turquoise water full of fish and other creatures. It widened as we went and no doubt grew deeper as well.

Something wasn't right. The further we went in the more we came across bits of the garden that needed digging over; patches – huge patches! – that needed planting and tending. We began to see half-finished buildings and small constructions that could have been works of art in the making. It wasn't always easy to tell what the intentions were, just that they weren't anywhere near finished. There were tools and brushes and strips of string and wire, alongside pots of colour and half-shaped bits of wood and clay and stone. There were beginnings of pictures etched on tree trunks or sketched in the dirt. Al went over and squatted down. He picked up a discarded chisel and began shaping a design on a tree trunk.

'Can he do that?' I said.

'D'you mean is he able to or is he allowed?' Isabeth said. She delicately wiped a single bead of perspiration from her forehead, then removed her jacket and laid it carefully over a branch. She gave me a cautious, shy smile.

'It's warm,' she said.

'You didn't answer my question,' I told her.

'Paradise is perfect. Not dull. God left the world unfinished, you know. So we could carry on. He started the process of creating and then handed things over to us. We're all creating all the time, don't you think? The question is – what are we making? And is it making the place better or worse?'

I had no answer. The concept was new to me. I'd always figured that Eden was a flawless place, which to be honest, made it sound a little uneventful. Apparently not.

2. Adventuring

A figure hurried by. I had to look twice but there was no mistaking it. The prophet in the bright blue baggy trousers and the crumpled flowery shirt. Ezekiel. He'd made it here too. I followed him. He went to a workshop of sorts, an open-fronted shelter made of branches and huge leaves interwoven. The structure itself was a work of art. Inside there was all sorts. As I loitered near the open front I watched him hard at work on a model of a city, made from precious stones. Gates, walls, buildings all constructed from blue, green and red gemstones. I doubt any of them were paste or fake. My guess is the thing was worth a fortune. He glanced up and smiled at me.

'Not bad, eh?' he said, and then he just carried on with his crafting.

I left him and wandered off again. As I turned a corner I nearly walked over Ruth and Esther, sat under a tree together. Ruth was strumming a guitar and Esther was making a kind of drum out of dried fruit skins, bark and a hollowed out tree stump. Ruth hummed to herself as she thumbed the strings. Esther added a subtle harmony. I backed away and listened for a while. The tune sounded familiar and it was a while before it came back to me. Then I got it. Jonah's song. There was a definite resemblance. But Ruth's voice was sweeter and Esther's a little more haunting.

I found Noah building another boat. Admittedly a good deal smaller and without, I presumed, the interference of warring neighbours. There were tools strewn everywhere, if anything the place looked more messy than when he'd been building the ark. He remembered me immediately and waved me over.

'Not another flood here, surely,' I said and he laughed and slapped the side of his creation with his coarse, flat hand.

'No, this is for adventuring. I hear the river broadens out further down so I'm taking my boys for another sail. See where it takes us. I'm told there are long-forgotten sea creatures and ancient aquatic monsters down there. Might bring a few back. You wanna come?'

I got the feeling I could have gone, but even in this paradise I still found myself reluctant to jump into the unknown. No doubt Al would have leapt at the chance, but I denied politely and went on my way.

Simon and his brother were playing some unrecognisable sport against James and John. It involved sticks, hoops, rackets and balls of various sizes, plus a lot of huffing and puffing. And every so often they stopped to argue about the score. There was clearly no lack of competitive spirit here, but the game never became antagonistic or vicious. They were at loggerheads and happy to be there. As I sat leaning on a rock I heard a familiar voice. The donkey had made it in too.

'I have a bone to pick with you,' I said.

'I know, I know,' the animal rolled his eyes and sat back on his back legs.

'You made an idiot out of me,' I said, 'there I was trying to convince Al about you, and what do you do? Impersonate an ordinary, no frills, dumb animal. Thanks a lot.'

'Well, you would have made an idiot of me. It was a serious moment and I wasn't about to turn it into an episode of the Muppets. Think what it would have looked like. I couldn't upstage the guy who designed everything could I? So I could talk, big deal. What's that when you put it alongside the guy who can calm storms, walk on water, and wrestle with death and win. And anyway, you got over it. Was probably a good lesson in humility for you.'

'Thanks. Good of you to take the time,' I mumbled.

'No problem,' he said, the sarcasm lost on him. 'Oh and to answer your question, I finished *Life of Pi*, I'm on *Trainspotting* now. It's a little different to *The Railway Children*, isn't it? Now I loved that. Well, I'd like to stick around chewing the fat all day, but I have to beat these guys at their own game. See ya.'

He started towards the fishermen and their unrecognisable sport.

'You mean – you can play this game?' I said.

'Of course. Who d'you think invented it?'

He bounded up to Simon and his mates, and threw his head back and brayed. The men stopped to look and at the same time three wolves, a young lion and a couple of sheep came hurtling out of the undergrowth. I leapt backwards and ran for cover. But they'd only come to join the game. By the time I walked away half a dozen animals had formed an opposing team and were beating Simon's lot hands down.

I passed Isaiah tuning his sports car and it was no rust bucket now. The thing gleamed in the sunlight, not a spot of corrosion in sight. I guess it didn't cough as it went along now. He grinned and nodded at me when he spotted me. Gave me a thumbs up and a 'Hey there pal!' as I went on by. I encountered them all again as I meandered around the place. Jeremiah, Abraham, Joshua, Rizpah, Gideon, Sarah, Abigail, Daniel. All of them. But they were somehow different. More peaceful, more at ease with themselves in this new world. Even Rahab. She just looked across and smiled as soon as she saw me. No recriminations, no cloud hanging there about that day we'd spent together and its strange, unfortunate end. I went over cautiously but she was keen to talk. I envied her as we chatted. Couldn't help it. She seemed free. Uncluttered. Her complex lifestyle a thing of the past. She'd left so much baggage behind. I wanted her to at least feel something about that brief time we'd spent together. But no. She was just happy. Content. We talked for a while and she laughed a lot, then I slipped away. Pleased for her but a little miserable for me. I had no idea how much time passed as I continued my wandering but eventually I dawdled into a clearing and found myself back with Isabeth and Aladdin.

3. Robbers

We hung out together for a good few hours. It may have been longer, there was little sense of time in the place. We threw ourselves in the glistening river and went for a good swim. When we worked up an appetite we draped ourselves on the bank and ate fruit we'd never tasted before. After that we had a go at making a few things. Al found a large, leathery piece of fruit and worked it into the shape of a football. We kicked it around and it lasted for a good few kickabouts. Isabeth was easily the brightest and best. I came a dull, distant third. No one cared. It was as we flopped down beside each other in a bundle of bodies and sweet-smelling sweat that we heard the jarring sound. The sound that broke the peace like a rock hurled through plate glass. The sound of shouting. Isabeth leapt up.

'Come on,' she said and she led us towards the noise.

The sound had carried quite away in the clear, clean air, so it took us a while to find them, but when we did we spotted them skulking in a ragged group not far from a grove of extraordinarily vibrant trees. The gang of rebels. We hung back at a safe distance and weighed the situation. The brute, who now appeared to be in charge, was ordering a few of the gang to plunder the nearby trees, along with some of the surrounding bushes and plants. They were grabbing handfuls of fruit, crushing it in their hurry and stuffing it in leather bags. Like nervous bank robbers scooping cash from a safe.

The sandwich maker was with them, looking a lot more dishevelled now. His hands were bound and Barn, the muscly guy with the flickering Adam's apple, was holding him by one arm.

'Which one?' the brute was saying.

The sandwich maker shook his head, so Barn pushed him onto his knees and presented a knife to his throat.

'Tell us,' the brute insisted.

'If you kill me you'll never know,' the sandwich maker said, his voice sounding strained and weaker than when we'd last heard him.

'It'll just take us longer, that's all. Sooner or later we'll find it.'

'Can they kill someone in paradise?' I whispered. Isabeth frowned and pursed her lips. 'I don't know,' she said softly.

There was a crash to the left of us and three of the rebels came at us through the undergrowth. We scattered but they were onto us and before we could fight back we found ourselves sprawling in the dirt at the feet of the brute. At least, being paradise, it was sweet dirt.

'I told you we'd catch up with you,' said the brute.

'I hate to correct you,' said Al, 'but we were the

ones who found you.'

The brute looked a little confused but let it pass. He gestured towards Barn who handed him the knife. The brute grabbed Isabeth with a fierce hand round her throat. He held her awkwardly and shoved the knife right onto her neck.

'Now you'll tell us,' he said. 'Unless you want her blood on your hands.'

The sandwich maker broke free from Barn's grip and stood up. He took his time, dusting his hands and knees. Isabeth's eyes were wide with panic. He locked his gaze on hers.

'All right,' he said, he had no choice now, she was his niece after all, flesh and blood. 'All right,' he said again. 'It's the third tree on the left there. You can't mistake it really. It's more vibrant and a whole lot more dense than the others.'

The brute nodded at Barn who took hold of the sandwich maker again and went looking in the grove. Isabeth was struggling to stay on her feet but she didn't dare crumble to her knees in case the knife cut into her flesh. I could see Al flexing his fingers, looking for all the world like he might wade in and save her at any minute.

'Yep,' Barn called a few seconds later, 'it's here all right.'

The brute let out a dark, savage laugh. 'The tree of life,' he said. 'There'll be no stopping us now. Lads, grab the bags and fill them with fruit, leaves, bark anything that'll come off it. Strip the thing.'

Isabeth gasped for breath and he let her go and threw her down.

'Ain't finished with you yet,' he said.

Al and I looked at each other. This wasn't good. The brute told a couple of the others to keep an eye on us and he went off after the others, in search of the tree of life. They herded us round a tree and made us sit down close together. Then they tore bits of fruit from a nearby tree and sat not far away munching on it.

'You okay?' I asked Isabeth.

She nodded but said nothing. She pressed a hand to her throat and massaged it a little.

'How about you?' Al said to the sandwich maker, 'you're looking a bit rough there.'

He forced a smile. 'Doing all right,' he said.

'Are we stuck here forever?' I asked.

'Not if they kill us all,' said Al and the sandwich maker laughed.

No one else did.

4. The Bag

I kept thinking that one of the others would drop by and rescue us. Simon or Samson or Joshua would have been good. One of the big guys. But no one came. I guess we had moved a fair distance from everyone when we were tracking this lot down. And now we were stranded.

'How did they get in here?' Isabeth asked as we sat huddled together, the two guards barely taking notice of us now.

The sandwich maker looked a little sheepish. 'I'm afraid I'm no brave man,' he said. 'They put pressure on me and I held out for a while, but in the end I made them what they needed.'

'What was that?' I asked.

He reached over to a discarded shoulder bag and pulled it close. We glanced at the guards but they couldn't have cared. He pulled out an old leather flask and removed the wad of cloth that was corking it. A few wisps of green smoke escaped.

'Will that get us out of here?' I said, but the sandwich maker shook his head.

'It's pretty much empty now. But I think there is a way,' he said. 'Isabeth, did you bring it?'

She nodded and reached for her jacket pocket. Her face changed suddenly, panic written deep in her expression.

'My jacket, I took it off back there. It's in the

pocket.'

No one said a word, I had no idea what they were talking about anyway. Al stuck a hand in the air.

'I'll go get it,' he said, but the sandwich maker shook his head.

'You go,' he said, looking at me.

'Me?' A scrum of fears collided in my mind at that moment. Fears about failing, death, weakness and looking the fool. I felt terrified and stupid and I was aware I was shaking my head repeatedly. I'd had a feeling a moment like this might come, I should have been more astute, more cautious, should have seen this coming. Now I was about to be unmasked for the coward I was, I'd been making attempts at playing the hero for a while, and somehow getting away with it, but it was a role I knew little about. It was a game I was bound to lose. So here I was, not getting away with it anymore. Isabeth put a hand on mine.

'You'll be fine,' she said, 'think about the dragon and everything else you've done so far.'

'But I... I...'

'We're all heroes and cowards really. We just hide it well. You're no weaker or stronger. You go.'

'What if I fail?' I said.

She shook her head, gave me that little smile again.

I stood up and my feet felt like lumps of iron. Too big, too heavy, too unwieldy for the rest of me. I didn't bother to look at the guards or hatch some wily excuse that I could offer them. I was too confused, too bewildered. I just turned and started walking away from the others. I wasn't even sure I could remember the way back. I just started because right then it was all I had the energy for, one dead, leaden foot in front of the other. I walked. I waited for the shouts, or the knife in the back, or the jagged rock clouting the back of my head. Nothing. Not even the wet splatter of ripe fruit on my neck. So I kept walking. And I kept walking. And I kept walking. I was still alive. So far.

5. Mighty Man

Maybe it was the nature of this garden, maybe there was someone else in control. Guiding my steps. Either way, sweating profusely and my heart pounding, I found myself back at the spot where Isabeth had given me that shy smile as she discarded her neat grey jacket. I ran to it and stood there, clutching my chest as I grabbed for every breath. I couldn't believe I'd made it this far. Why wasn't I dead or injured or being pummelled with rocks or something? I looked back. I was alone. Very alone. I wondered how long it would take to track down some help, to find the likes of Ezekiel, James, Noah and his sons or Abigail. Ruth, she was resourceful and brave. Where was she?

Silence. No sign of anyone. I was desperate for some backup, but I didn't dare call out in case the rebels were looking for me and I gave my position away. I looked around frantically, sweat trickling into my eyes. I could of course just keep running. Make for the gates and never look back. Save my skin and leave the others to make a way out. They were resourceful enough, for Gandalf's sake, they were far better equipped than I was to fight their way out of this predicament. I was the weak link, the sad case. Perhaps this was a God-given chance for me to make my escape. I stared at the jacket again and stood there, torn in two. Eventually, ever so slowly, I picked it up and patted the pockets. One of them bulged with the packet Isabeth had picked up on her way out of the train. I draped the jacket over my arm and turned around.

'See,' said a voice, 'you can do it.'

I looked back at her. The woman in white with the rosy cheeks and the short black hair. I wasn't really surprised to see her. Everyone else seemed to be there. But I was scared as hell that she might have been reading my mind. Did she have the power to do that?

'I haven't made it back yet,' I said.

'You'll be all right... Mighty Man,' she said. 'Think of all those other people you rescued along the way.'

'I didn't rescue anyone.'

'You may not think you did. But that doesn't change anything.' She paused. 'I gave him the nudge you know.'

'Who?'

'The sandwich maker, that night on the bridge. He was in two minds about where to go for a walk, so I tweaked his decision making. Nudged him towards the bridge. He rescued you, now you can rescue him.' I stared at her. Everyone else seemed to know far more about what was going on than I did.

'Don't look so worried. I'll see you around.'

And she walked away, just a few steps, then she seemed to melt in the air, like a wisp of divine smoke, carried away.

So there it was. I could still run. I could do it. Get

away. Be free. The option was lying there, like an open door in front of me. I could do it. I turned back and tried to retrace my steps. I got lost twice but eventually spotted the two guards leaning on each other, looking bored out of their minds. They sharpened up the moment they saw me.

'Where've you been?' one of them flared up, he was as a thin as a twig and his face made me think of an emaciated ferret.

'One more stupid move like that and you'll never walk again,' he barked, and he cleared his throat and spat at me.

I dodged the missile and ran over to the others.

Al grinned like a kid with an ice cream and punched my arm.

'You had me going for a while,' he said, 'I wondered if I'd see you again.'

Isabeth just nodded, took the jacket and pulled out the packet. She handed it to the sandwich maker. He unwrapped it and took out a small loaf of bread and a little silver flask.

'I went back for that?' I said. 'A bit of food and drink?' I couldn't believe it.

'It's more than food and drink,' he said. 'I got this from the feast on the hill,' he held up the bread, 'and I got this,' he waved the flask, 'from the wedding.'

He laid them on a rock.

'Divine bread and wine,' he said.

'You were there?' I said. 'At that feast on the hill?'

'Absolutely. And at Cana. At that wedding.'
He bowed his head for a moment and whispered a few quiet words then he looked at us, took hold of the bread and broke it up. He handed a lump to each of us. I glanced at the guards, they were watching but not caring. In the background I could still hear the rest of the rebels, arguing and insulting one another.

'Let's eat,' said the sandwich maker, and we swallowed the bread.

I'd like to tell you it tasted like the best bread in the world, but it didn't. Not really. It was regular bread, it was fresh and it tasted fine.

'Why are we doing this?' I said.

'It's the way back. You'll find the warriors will let you pass.'

The warriors?

'And it's the last meal I'll ever serve.'

Isabeth grabbed her uncle's arm. 'What do you mean?' she said. 'What are you talking about?'

'I'm not coming,' he said, and he offered her the flask of wine. 'No need. My job's done. I'm staying here.' His voice was flat and matter of fact. As if there was nothing unusual about what he was saying. Nothing heroic.

'But what about the rebels? They'll kill you,' Al said.

The sandwich maker ignored this. Instead he encouraged Isabeth to drink. She tipped the wine to her lips and then passed it to Al.

He tipped it recklessly and a few drops traced a line down his chin.

I took the flask and drank a mouthful. That wasn't ordinary. It was good wine. Very good wine. The sandwich maker took it from us and drained it.

'Don't waste this experience' he said quietly, 'any of you. Do your best to draw on it every day.'

He slipped the flask back inside the canvas packet. He stood up and encouraged the rest of us to do the same. The guards took notice of that.

6. Burning Up

'Where are you going?' the skinny one called.

The sandwich maker urged us to start walking away. 'Go,' he said, with a world of insistence in that single word.

The voices of the rest of the gang were growing louder, they were coming back from raiding the tree of life.

'Go!' he said to us again.

We started walking. The sandwich maker approached the two guards.

'You have me,' he said, 'you don't need them.'

'Wait a minute...'

The other rebels started to appear now.

'Run!' the sandwich maker said.

Al started to run. The brute saw us getting away and grabbed the sandwich maker. We saw the flash of his knife. He dragged him towards us.

'If you run I'll kill him,' he snarled.

'It'll do you no good,' said the sandwich maker.

There was a sudden yelp from one of the gang. Smoke was rising from one of the bags of gathered fruit.

'What the...?'

The brute threw down the sandwich maker and picked up the bag. Flames engulfed his hand and he hurled it down again. The other bags started smouldering too.

'You can't steal from this garden,' the sandwich maker said.

'Yes we can,' said Barn. 'Get it out of the bags, boys. Get the fruit.'

The gang began ripping open their bags, trying to retrieve the furiously smoking fruit.

'Get going!' yelled the sandwich maker to us.

We stayed at a distance but didn't move.

The gang hurled the burning bags away and grabbed at nearby rocks.

'What magic is this?' the brute barked, 'I always knew you were dangerous, what curse have you put on this fruit.'

'It's not me, there's no curse. But you can't take it out of here and use it for destruction. It has the blessing of God on it.'

'You're lying!' the brute screamed and his face contorted and filled up with a deep shade of purple fury. 'Finish him lads.' He ordered and he lifted a rock way over his head.

Barn slapped the sandwich maker's face, knocking his thick antenna glasses off and into some nearby bushes. Then he grabbed the sandwich maker's white coat and tore it off, a symbolic stripping of his power and some kind of clumsy attempt at humiliation. Then he stood there, watching, a cruel smile on his lips, the white coat draped over his arm.

What followed was the worst thing I'd seen in the whole adventure. The most sickening, harrowing moment. There was something other-worldly about that extraordinary man as he mumbled a quiet prayer, then lifted his face towards his enemies. The gang stood poised with fistfuls of rocks and smouldering fruit.

'No!' screamed Isabeth.

The sandwich maker looked towards us, gave us a final smile, and closed his eyes slowly. It was almost as if he had surrendered his spirit before they'd thrown a single stone. And throw them they did. Rock after rock, fire on fire. The sound was appalling and still rings in my head sometimes. Al grabbed Isabeth's face and turned it away. I watched in unbelief. The rebels dispensing death as if they were machines. Nothing human about the way they pounded him, time and again. Minute after minute after minute. Never giving up until there was nothing left to see but a jagged, brutal pile of red rocks, and a pool of the sandwich maker's blood seeping out towards their shoes.

'Let's get out of here,' Al snapped, his voice a strange mixture of horror and anger.

I grabbed Isabeth and Al grabbed me and we ran for our lives.

'Oh no you don't,' the brute called after us. 'Get them.'

I half expected a shower of rocks and burning fruit to come hailing down upon us, but maybe they had tired of that particular bloodsport. Instead their feet pounded the ground and they headed our way. We just kept going, no idea of the right path home, we just had to keep moving, and hopefully faster than the rebels.

7. Warriors

Al saw them first, two huge dazzling warriors, both armed with colossal flaming swords. They were stationed in front of the gate, blocking the way out. We were trapped.

'What now?' I said as Al grabbed us and we stopped running.

We looked back, the gang had been gaining on us and were close now.

'Scatter,' said Al, and we split three ways.

The rebels spotted the warriors and slowed up, they grouped together and picked up a few missiles.

'This looks like trouble,' said the brute.

The warriors said nothing.

Al was standing as close as he dared to the one on the right, I was near the one on the left. Isabeth had taken refuge in a nearby olive grove.

The brute took a few steps forward, and some of the gang followed. Some of them had splashes of the sandwich maker's blood on their hands and faces. The warriors shifted position and angled their blades towards them.

'Right,' said the brute, 'Let's do it. They can't take us all.'

But they could. And they did. The rebels ran at them hurling their rocks as they came, but the warriors merely batted the missiles away as if swatting flies. Nothing made contact. And when the first rebels came within striking distance of the flaming swords they were cut down with a single slice, six or seven at a time. The warriors were around eight or nine feet in height so the rebels were never going to trouble them. A few swings of the burning blades and the insurgents were left dead or reeling. In the end, and it wasn't long coming, there was only Barn and the skinny guard left. The skinny guy started to protest but Barn shut him up and they two of them fell on their knees and bowed their heads, waiting for the blade to finish them. They stayed there for a long time but the end was slow in coming. The warriors lowered their swords and turned their eyes on us.

'You can pass,' said the one on the left, and we flinched at the extraordinary sound of his voice. Like a bunch of voices speaking in harmony. The other warrior nodded agreement, though his eyes still blazed with fire as he monitored us.

'You're sure?' I said, and even as I said it I couldn't quite believe I was checking with him.

They said nothing more, they didn't even nod.

So we came together, met in front of them and took the risk of weaving between them. The heat from the swords caught our faces as we went past. It was as if someone had just opened a furnace. We sped up and went through the gates. When we looked back Barn and the skinny guy were still on the floor, kneeling and waiting. And then the flash came. That was the best way to describe it really.

A light burst through the sky above our heads and we got the briefest glimpse of a throne made of blue sapphire. For a moment I saw a figure the colour of gleaming amber. There was a halo around him, like a rainbow shining through the clouds. And his eyes were shimmering like jewels reflecting a roaring fire. His feet shone like polished bronze and there were stars in the palm of his hand. I could barely look at his face it was so brilliant and radiant, like staring at the sun on midsummer's day.

I say I saw all this but to be honest it was so brief and fleeting that I may have imagined it, and to this day I have never checked with the others to see if they saw the same thing.

8. Vacuum

After that we were suddenly back in the sandwich maker's back room. The same smell of food in the air. We looked at each other and could say nothing. It was as if an unspoken agreement passed between us. A bond forged in the heat of that odyssey. Isabeth's eyes welled up with tears and Al put an arm around her. I could feel myself tearing up too, so I did the manly thing and looked away. I went out into the shop and walked around picking things up and putting them down again. I barely knew him really. But he'd saved my life. Twice. I pulled out my smart phone. It immediately came back to life. The contraption had somehow survived dragon attack, flood waters and countless other mishaps not covered by the warranty. As had I.

The next weeks were a strange time. I felt as if I was living in a sort of vacuum between the gloom of normal life, which would surely never be more than a pale imitation now, and the memories of that shocking, swashbuckling, terrifying, exhilarating adventure. Every night I dreamt about it, sometimes back in paradise, at other times fleeing the dragon. Some nights I found myself cradling that baby in my arms, at other times I was standing staring at that distant figure suspended on that grim hill. There was one dream I never had again though. The one about the night I had been mugged then rescued by the sandwich maker. That was done and dusted now. I did revisit the bridge, and I stood in that same spot where I'd plotted to jump. And in going back there I found that I'd changed, there was nothing left of the urge to end it now. That was a part of me I couldn't locate any more. The despair had gone.

9. What I Needed

And so, sitting in that stale old armchair I finished telling him all this, more than I'd ever intended, and I waited for his reaction. This was supposed to be a business deal, not a therapy session. Still, it had done me no harm. He held out his open hand and I passed him the leather pouch. He opened it and gingerly fingered the very green leaves.

'So that was all a highly longwinded way of explaining how you came by these,' he said. 'Hmm.'
He rubbed them gently, smelt his fingers. A few minutes went by, during which he did nothing but examine the leaves. 'I have to say I've never come across anything like these before,' he said, eventually breaking the silence, 'the colour, the texture, the aroma. All quite unique. Quite unique.'

He held them up to the light. 'I'd have to send them off for testing of course.' He smiled for the first time. 'And you say you got these in…' he hesitated, couldn't bring himself to say it, so I finished the sentence for him.

'In paradise. In the first garden. Off one of the most dynamic trees you could ever want to see.'

He studied them again, then he studied me.

'In paradise? You mean like an island somewhere?

'No I mean paradise. In another world somewhere.'

He shook his head, clearly unconvinced.

'Well, I don't buy it, but if there's anything close to truth in it, these could be worth a fortune. Would certainly make you famous. Articles, news stories, interviews, a documentary perhaps. You could become a celebrity overnight. If these are halfway genuine.'

'How can you ever prove that?' I said.

He shrugged. 'It would be enough to prove they are not from anywhere else.'

I looked down again at my moleskine diary. The thing was stuffed full of my notes and scribblings.

'And you say you've had these for two months now, and they still haven't faded or lost their vibrancy.'

I shook my head.

'Extraordinary,' he said.

'Yes,' I said, 'they are extraordinary.'

'If these did come from... where you say... I'm surprised you were able to take them away with you.'

I sighed. 'Well, to be honest, others tried and they... well, they failed.'

For a moment my mind flashbacked to the images of the burning bags.

'Your life could never be the same again, you know,' he went on.

I held up the notebook and thought about the sandwich maker and his last meal.

'You know – it already has changed. I'm dead sure I'll never be the same.'

He forced a smile. 'Fair enough,' he said.

I reached out and took the leaves and the pouch back.

'I'll leave it for now,' I said.

'What? But... you can't do that. We're closing a deal here. I thought you said you needed the cash?'

'I do. I'm about to start training to be a priest and money's going to be tight for a while.'

'Well, with what you get for these you could probably train for the next decade.'

I looked at the leaves. It was a tempting prospect. I'd been wondering how I'd pay my way. More than that. I'd been praying for a solution. Knocking on heaven's door. Maybe this was the answer. I started to cave in. Then an image flashed through my head, a vision of newspaper headlines and distorted tales of magic wonder leaves. I thought of the doomed rebels with their hands full of stolen, smouldering fruit and Jeremiah thrown down that well for his faithfulness. I guessed he would never have sold leaves from paradise for an easier life.

I tucked them back into the pouch and slipped them into my pocket.

'It's tempting,' I said, 'but you know – there'll be another way. I'm sure. I think I'll hang on to these.'

And I turned and left his office. He was still protesting as the door shut but I didn't turn back.

Outside Aladdin was sitting on a bench, playing a game on his phone.

'At last,' he said. 'I thought he'd bumped you off in there. By the way. Isabeth just texted, she wants to know if you've got your best man speech sorted for Saturday? She's got a mind like a vice that woman. Nothing's going to be left to chance.'

'I'll be ready,' I said. 'How about you?'

He grinned. 'I told you she was my type,' he said.

'No, I believe you said she wasn't your type.'

'Yea, but opposites attract, right?' He punched my arm. 'Anyway. What's the news? You were in there forever with that dude. You get what you wanted? Our dodgy botanist friend come through for you?'

'You know I think he did, Al,' I said, 'I got what I needed.'

The End

A Few Bible References

Part One

3.	Ezekiel	Ezekiel chapter 37
4.	Noah	Genesis chapter 6
5.	Deborah	Judges chapter 4
6.	Joshua	Joshua chapter 5
7.	Abram	Genesis chapter 14
8.	Rizpah	2 Samuel chapter 21
9.	Ruth	Ruth chapter 1
10.	The Animal	Numbers chapter 22
11.	Jeremiah	Jeremiah chapter 38
12.	The Woman in White	1 Kings chapter 19
13.	Joseph	Genesis chapter 37
14.	Rahab	Joshua chapter 2
15.	Ehud	Judges chapter 3
16.	Sarah	Genesis chapter 18
17.	Gideon	Judges chapter 6
18.	Isaiah	Isaiah chapters 9, 11, 20 & 43
19.	Daniel	Daniel chapter 6
20.	Ezekiel again	Ezekiel chapter 47
21.	Esther	Esther chapter 7
22.	Shiphrah, Puah & Moses	Exodus chapters 1 & 2
23.	Abigail	1 Samuel chapter 25
24.	Samson	Judges chapters 13–16
25.	Jonah	Jonah chapters 1–4

Part Two

3.	The Creature	Revelation chapter 12
4.	The Stranger	Luke chapters 4 & 5
5.	The Hillside	John chapter 6
7.	The Mountain	Matthew chapter 17
9.	The Parade	Matthew chapter 21
10.	The Dream	Luke chapter 10
11.	The Thunder	Exodus chapters 19 & 24
12.	The Graveyard	Luke chapter 23
13.	The Glory	Luke chapter 24

Part Three

1.	Unfinished	Genesis chapter 1 & Revelation chapter 21
7.	Warriors	Revelation chapter 1

Printed in Great Britain
by Amazon.co.uk, Ltd.,
Marston Gate.